FLOWERS HONOR OUR LOVES, OUR

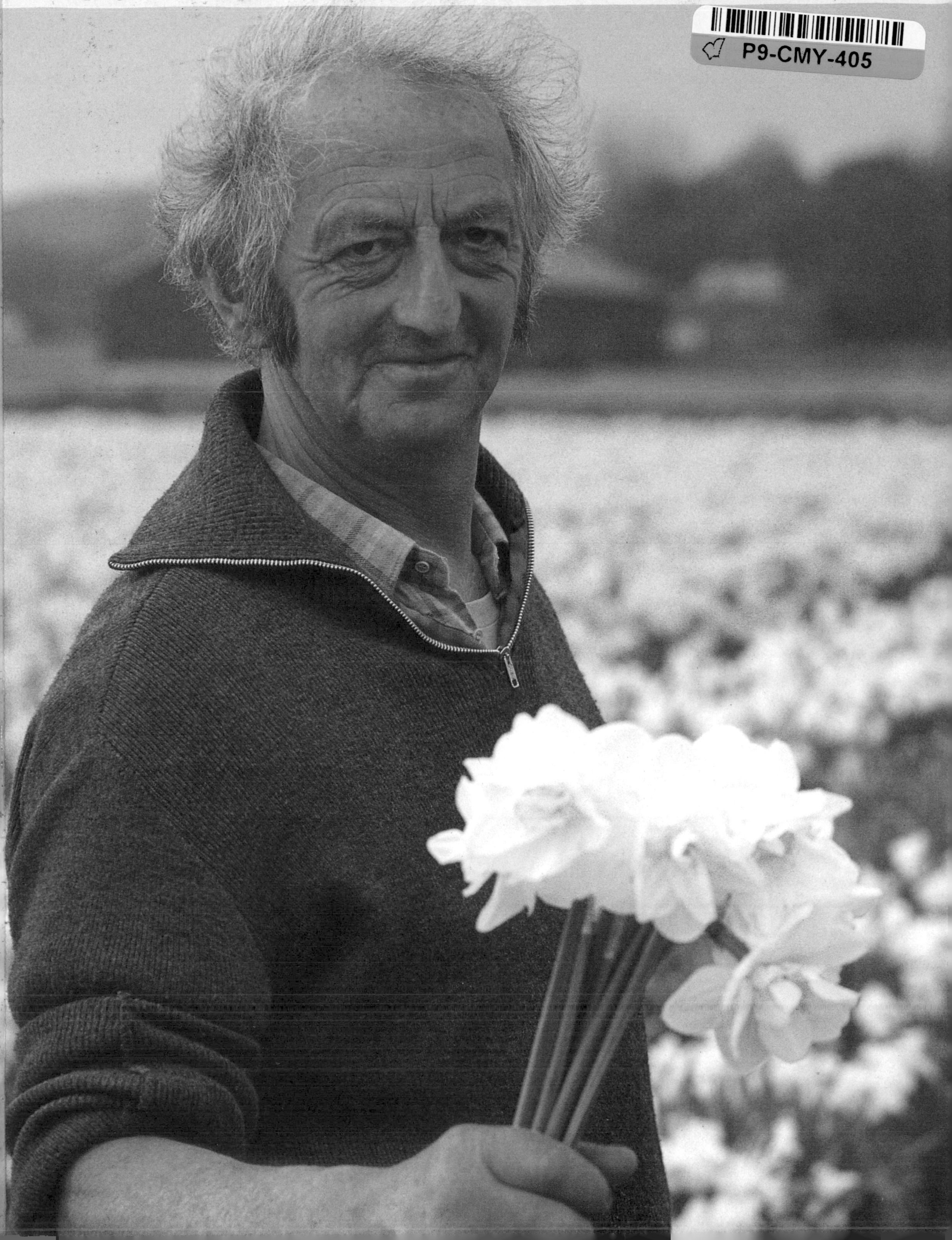

CLOSE TO THE FACE OF NATURE.

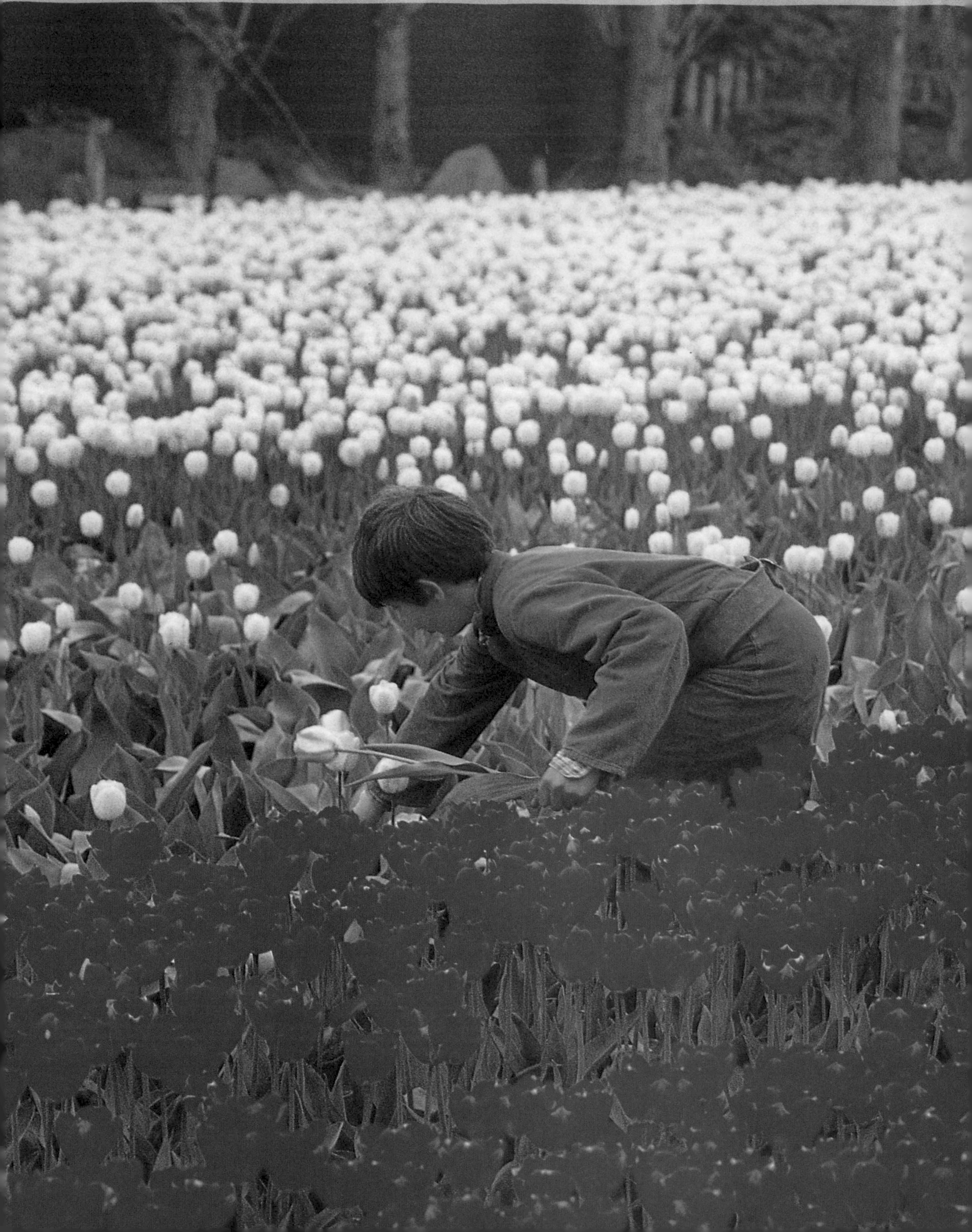

FOR THOSE WHO WATCH, FLOWERS

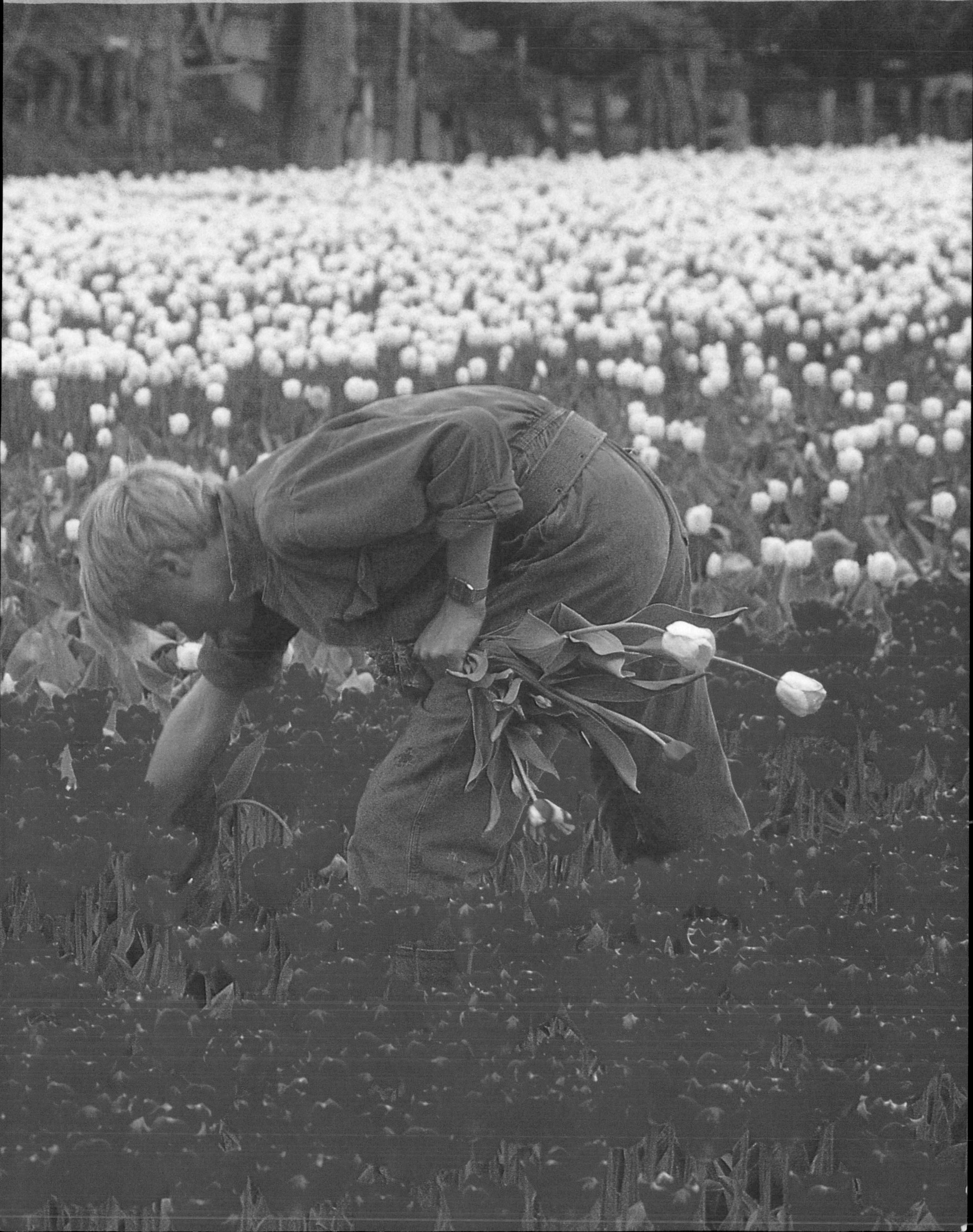

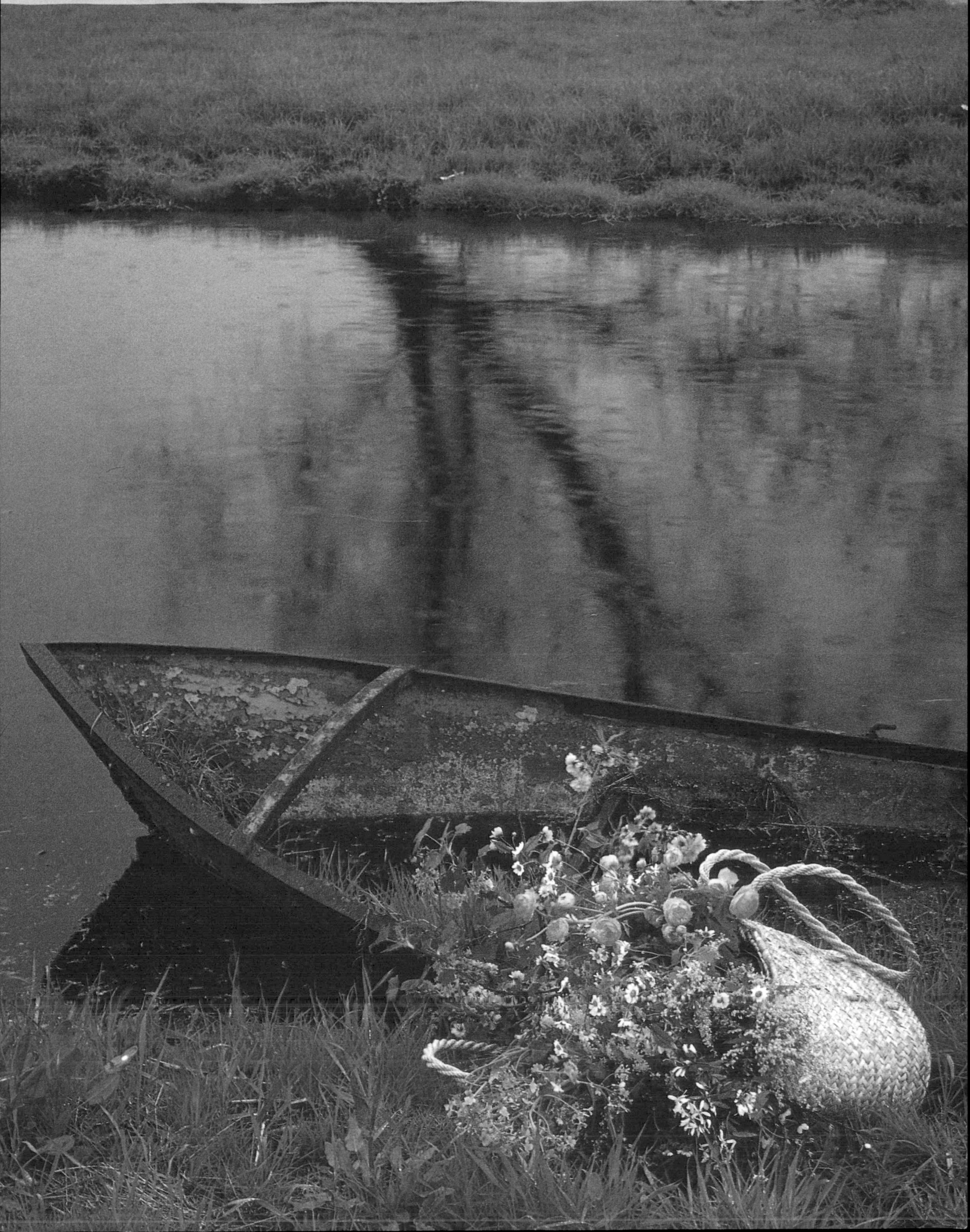

DIE AND LIVE WITH US.

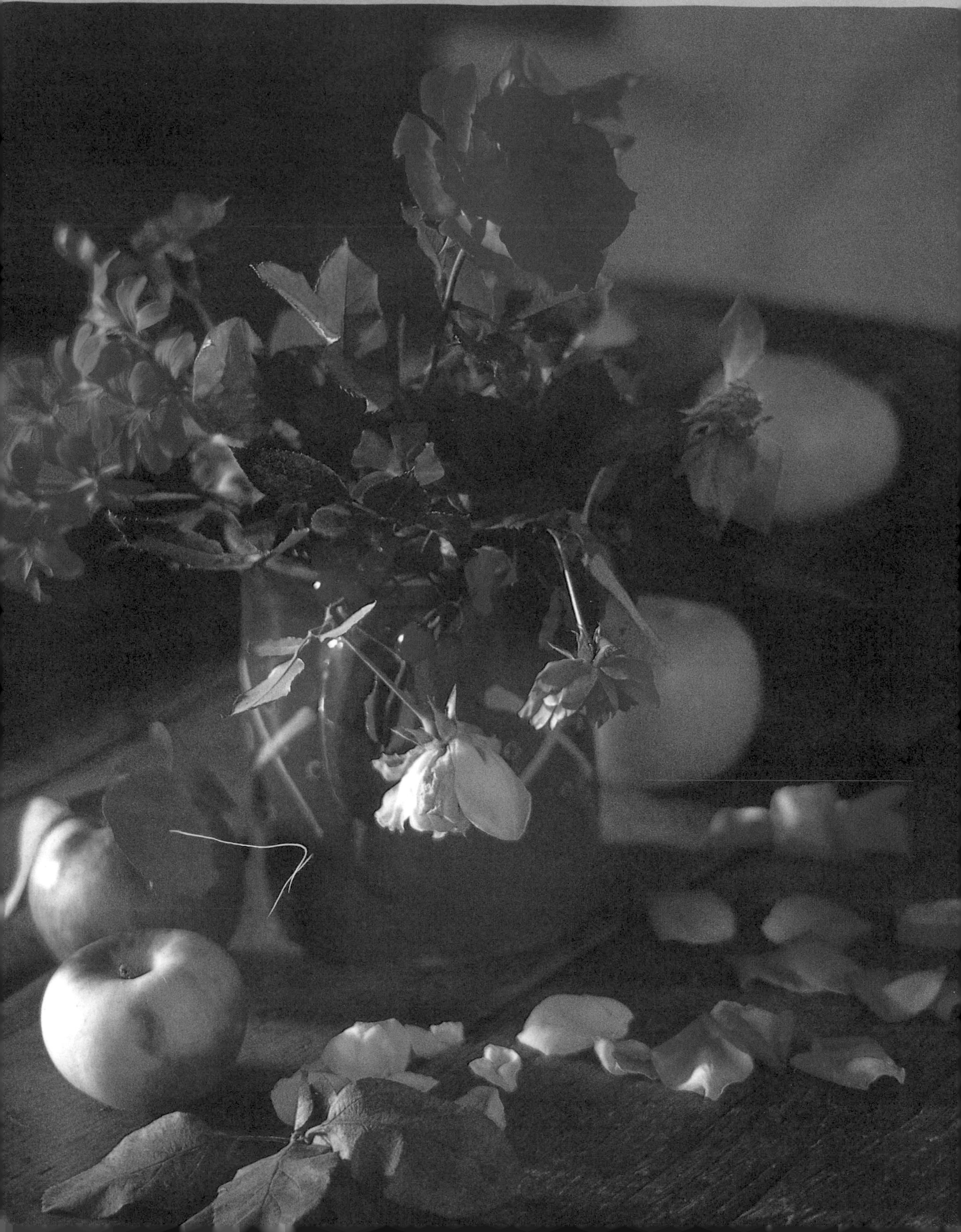

MÄDDERLAKE'S

TRADE SECRETS

NEW YORK

CLARKSON POTTER/PUBLISHERS

Tom Pritchard and Billy Jarecki

FINDING AND ARRANGING FLOWERS NATURALLY

PHOTOGRAPHS BY LANGDON CLAY
AND TOM PRITCHARD

MÄDDERLAKE'S TRADE SECRETS

A complete list of photograph credits appears on page 184.

Copyright ©1994 by Pure Mädderlake Ltd.

Photographs copyright © 1994 by Langdon Clay

Photographs copyright © 1994 by Tom Pritchard

Published by Clarkson N. Potter, Inc., 201 East 50th Street, New York, New York 10022.

Member of the Crown Publishing Group.

Random House, Inc. New York, Toronto, London, Sydney, Auckland.

CLARKSON N. POTTER, POTTER, and colophon are trademarks of Clarkson N. Potter, Inc.

Manufactured in China

DESIGN BY JANE TREUHAFT

Library of Congress Cataloging-in-Publication Data

Pritchard, Tom.
Trade secrets: finding and arranging flowers naturally; Tom Pritchard and Billy Jarecki.
p. cm.
Includes index.
1. Flower arrangement. 2. Pure Mädderlake (Firm) 3. Cut flower industry.
I. Jarecki, Billy. II. Pure Mädderlake (Firm) III. Title.
SB449.P73 1994
745.92—dc20   92-29775
ISBN 0-517-59332-7 (cloth)
ISBN 0-517-88158-6 (paper)
10 9 8 7 6 5 4 3 2 1
FIRST EDITION

FRONTISPIECE: *Anything that holds water can hold flowers. A geranium flower carefully lodged in a sherry glass provides an anchor for cuttings from Japanese kerria, columbine, wood hyacinth, wild rose, and nasturtiums.*

[A word of Thanks]

Trade Secrets has taken over seven years to discover and produce. We thank the following for helping us along the way:

IN ENGLAND AND SCOTLAND: The Chelsea Flower Show; Lord and Lady Leigh at Stoneleigh Abbey; Eve Molesworth at The Orangery; Giles and Roz Weaver at Greywalls.

IN HOLLAND: The Verenigde Bloemenveilingen Aalsmeer; Keukenhof Gardens; The Kasteel- Museum, Sypesteyn, Nieuw-Loosdrecht; Harry Mesterom and Robert Buys.

IN FRANCE: Musee Monet at Giverny; Mr. and Mrs. Raymond Humbert at Musee Rural des Art Populaires; The Wholesale Flower Terminal at Rungis; Christian Badin; Mr. and Mrs. Fraise; Annie Chazottes, Anne and Julien; Simon and Julie Fletcher; Le Passé Simple; Lilian François; Moulie Savart.

IN ITALY: Gil Cohen and Paul Gervais; Peter Page and Leonardo Marchini; Bea Sagar, John Kelly, and Huck Snyder.

IN JAPAN: The Tokyo Wholesale Flower Market; Isamu Miyake at The Miyake Nursery; Takaaki Nonen.

IN KENYA: The Mount Kenya Safari Club.

IN SAVANNAH: Jim Williams; Judy Bradley; Magnolia Place.

IN WASHINGTON, D.C.: The National Gallery of Art.

IN NEW YORK CITY: Amanda Coleman; Calvin Klein; Evelyn Lauder; The Central Synagogue; The Royalton Hotel; The 21 Club; Amy Rome at The New York City Ballet.

THE PEOPLE WHO HELP US GET THE MOST OUT OF THE NEW YORK FLOWER MARKET: Ben Fischer, Gary Page, Kevin Esteban at Fischer and Page; Jim Weisse and Mac Ayoubi at Caribbean Cuts; Rob and Dick Houtenbos, Piet and Cees Lozer, Cas Trap, Hans Schoutsen, Ibrahim Kalil, Carl Grimes at Dutch Flower Line; Earl and Daniel at Hatleberge-de Castro Orchids; Henry at Evans Nurseries; Steven Boehl at S.S.F. Flowers, and Hillary Bruno.

IN THE UNION SQUARE FARMER'S MARKET: James Durr, Dumitru Farms.

THE NURSERIES: Brookville Nursery; Martin Viette Nursery; Meadow-brook Farms; Nabel's Nursery; Ott's Exotic Plants; The Rhoads Garden; Samuel Bridge Nursery; Sprainbrook Nursery; Tuccinardi Garden Center; Waterloo Gardens.

AT PURE MÄDDERLAKE: Jim Wilson and Robert Pesany.

MY AGENT: Lew Grimes.

AT CLARKSON POTTER: My editor, Roy Finamore; Esther Sam; my designer, Jane Treuhaft; Howard Klein; Michelle Sidrane; Lauren Shakely; Amy Boorstein; Joan Denman.

Special thanks to Michael Geiger, Brian Hagiwara, Lee Bailey, Ken Druse, Timothy Mawson, Alice Waters, Linda Yang, and to Heidi Gurbarg for her cutting list. Heidi has now created her own flower and gift store, Natural Creations, in Chestnut Ridge, NY.

CONTENTS

A LETTER TO

I am writing Trade Secrets for you guys. From the looks of things, you're off to a good, if somewhat shaky, start. But it is a start.

Although much of this book addresses how to find the widest range of flowers and presents the best ideas we've found for working with them, I think it's useful to consider what makes the flower business unlike any other before you go off trying to figure out its practical side. If you were going to become grocers, I'd say plunge headlong into the marketplace and learn how to buy the best and the freshest lettuces and vegetables you could possibly find. But to become a florist, you must first recognize and embrace the fact that flowers have been called upon by cultures spanning the globe and the centuries to represent the deepest and most vital feelings we each can have. In other words, in addition to being beautiful objects in and of themselves, flowers are also capable of transcending their simple physical description and embodying higher purpose. Bearing that in mind, I've tried to jot down all the things I can think of that flowers can do or might be called upon to convey.

➤ Fresh flowers are a presence to be felt and enjoyed, a means we all have to elaborate our surroundings and make them more than they were without flowers.

THREE YOUNG BOYS

- Flowers can be markers of welcome, of greeting, of thanks.
- Flowers help us celebrate the happiest days of our lives. From the joyous occasion of a brand-new life through the rituals of coming of age to the union of one life with another—we call upon flowers to make our most important moments memorable.
- By their presence in our surroundings, flowers can help connect us to the natural world many of us have all but locked out of our lives.
- By their ability to trigger associations, flowers help reconnect us to meaningful times, events, or places from our past.
- When we recognize and accept their own mortal presence, flowers help remind us of the natural ebb and flow of life, the very notion that death is an acceptable and integral part of living.
- Finally, perhaps more eloquently than our words ever could, flowers can represent and convey our deepest feelings of love.

That said, you guys must also recognize that the flowers available to most of us today are not capable of bearing out such heady promise. Our current view of how we define and use fresh flowers is archaic. For reasons described in the chapters that follow, we have collectively narrowed our flower choices to but a meager few, standardized the ways we assemble them, and failed to realize that in so doing we have subverted the very qualities in flowers we claim to revere.

Much needs to be done to wake up a sleeping industry and chart a course to more favorable winds. Trade Secrets describes how.

tom pritchard

PURE MÄDDERLAKE

THE STORE EXPOSED

[*Part One*]

A QUICK LOOK BACK

FROM THE BEGINNING, Mädderlake challenged the assumptions and traditions of the floral industry. Everywhere we looked, we were bothered by what we saw: a flower-selling system that was set up to deliver but the palest reflection of the bounty of nature; florists engaged in formulaic work; customers who didn't seem to care about what they got, happy just to get something. We were convinced it didn't have to be so and set out to discover how to find and fashion truly gorgeous flowers and how to use them in a variety of settings.

We quickly learned that we were *not* floral decorators, that we did not see flowers just as a way to dress up an interior. We looked to flowers for something much deeper than that, and finally understood, after years of working with them, that, for us, flowers represent missing pieces of nature. Since so many of us live so unconnected to the natural world, the right flowers, flowers that accurately reflect the beauty of the natural world, can help us restore an imbalance we have unwittingly created in our own surroundings.

Because so many of the florist's flowers we encountered in the mar-

kets didn't even begin to fill that bill, we looked to farmer's markets and nurseries, woods and gardens for our raw materials. This quest for extraordinary material often called for two or three weekly trips to greenhouses and gardens in the near and far countryside, and finally led us to conclude that **THE INITIAL CHOICE OF FLOWERS IS THE SINGLE MOST IMPORTANT STEP IN THE MÄDDERLAKE FLOWER-ARRANGING PROCESS.**

As we were not schooled in the art of floral design, we were able to fashion our own approach to flower arranging. We realized that universal ideas that pertain to architecture and environment—notions of space, form, line, and texture—inform the floral arts as well. In fact, we reasoned that all creative projects, no matter what format or purpose, answer to the same criteria. And although we may have developed a discernible floral style over the years, we have learned to take nothing for granted, to question all assumptions before accepting any of them. It is only with a complete questioning and understanding of the "why" that we can really find the "how." Otherwise, we're just repeating or copying.

PREVIOUS PAGES: *Why must florists' coolers be identical? In our SoHo store, we made ours into a little indoor building complete with French doors, and lodged it front and center. Don't limit your choices! The Alka Seltzer "vase" makes a delightfully unexpected holder for a foxglove.*

ABOVE: *Billy and I complete frantic preparations for the first customer in our about-to-open Village store.* **RIGHT:** *Across the shop, funny green water lettuce float amid pots of papyrus in our sunny little water garden.* **OPPOSITE:** *The elegant "flower box" in our second uptown shop.*

In addition to the natural flower mixes that have become our signature, our work has been scattered over a wide range of territory and has summoned up all the skills and ideas we could muster. Our architectural projects include the transformation of a former New York City equestrian rink into a school and rehearsal space for the American Ballet Theater; the creation in the Catskills of a house and dance studio wrapped entirely in black rubber; and a house to be built in an ancient olive grove at the base of the monastery walls that crown the Greek island of Patmos.

Our forays into landscaping began with a terrace and roof garden in Toronto, which took two years to complete and led me as far as the Sacramento Valley in California to find the most appropriate material. With the architect Tod Williams we tackled the transformation of an island retreat off the shores of Darien, from fanciful and decidedly Italianate to the natural tangle of the Connecticut wilds. We restored the natural landscape obliterated by construction equipment at Calvin and Kelly Klein's rambling house in East Hampton, New York, making it impossible to discern that anything around the house had ever been disturbed. And we created a natural swimming pool lodged into an exposed shelf of ledgerock on a spectacular site in Greenwich, Connecticut.

Although we rarely compete for social-event work, we have produced some innovative settings for special occasions over the years. Our ideas and designs have graced New York's Pierpont Morgan Library, Yale's British Arts Centre, and the White House. For our biggest bash, a party for 4,000 to celebrate *A Chorus Line*'s achievement of "longest running Broadway musical" status, flowers were but a footnote. Five tents, thousands of chasing lights, endless panels of mirrors, a two-story marquee and stage, and weeks of work combined to produce the glamorous Hollywood setting we had conceived for the glittering array of guests who were to pour into Shubert Alley for the celebration.

Vibrant flowers *were* center stage in the intimate "secret garden" setting we fashioned for the opening night of the *Treasure Houses of Britain* exhibition at the National Gallery of Art in Washington, D.C. Harsh November winds howling outside the massive gallery building were supplanted by a tender summer breeze indoors. Tall, trellised walls (trucked down from New York) harbored a garden dominated by a fountain filled with water lilies and surrounded by a glorious border of full-blown summer flowers. Candles sheltered by hurricane shades edged pathways, ringed the fountain, and cast a warm, welcome glow everywhere.

We always attempt to go beyond what is required, to think as fully and completely about each task at hand and to develop as interesting and fresh a response as we possibly can. When you begin to shovel out a product, the promise of freshness and invention is severely compromised, no matter what the medium.

A number of houses have sheltered our pursuits. Our journey began in a somewhat scruffy but charming little corner store in Greenwich Village. Within a year or so we moved uptown to a very chic address on Madison Avenue directly across from Halston's bustling fashion emporium, then sidestepped a few years later to two floors of a townhouse just off Madison. Our latest move has plunked us down squarely in the middle of SoHo. Each move helped us grow to another place in our

evolving career: the Village shop gave us our sea legs and a chance to explore the territory; Madison Avenue brought us fame, national press, and superstar clients; and 73rd Street was home base for the creation of our first book, *Flowers Rediscovered*, as well as for the growth of our landscape and event business. Our current Broadway store takes us in another direction. Our move to SoHo—long the domain of artists, but recently home to a multitude of advertising agencies, publishers, architects, and designers of all kinds—coincides with a desire on our part to put ourselves in close touch with the creative energy of New York and, in addition to our continuing work with flowers, to pursue our interests in writing, architecture and interior design, home furnishings, and photography.

GENESIS

THERE IS NOTHING MORE IMPORTANT to any florist or flower lover than to have an abundant and ever-changing selection of extraordinary flowers with which to work. Sadly, this situation rarely exists for any of us, anywhere. Until these circumstances change, you will need to sharpen your discovery skills and look in a variety of places for your bounty.

The Need to Be Resourceful

When we first began, we often worked eleven and twelve hours a day to keep our store filled with beautiful plants and flowers, and went to great lengths to get them. Since the kinds of flower arrangements we had conjured up in our mind's eye could not be made from just what we could find in New York City's flower markets, we undertook long trips away from the city to find and assemble such an extensive selection.

On a recent visit to Venice, it suddenly dawned on us—after years of using them for cut flowers—why these particular tumbling geraniums were named "balcon" hybrids.

One day I might drive the length of Long Island and raid the dozens of nurseries and garden centers scattered about the Hamptons and Amagansett; another would find me just north of Philadelphia, ready for a hard day's run through the Schuylkill and Delaware valleys, hitting a succession of thirty or more establishments; a more frequent target somewhat closer to the city was Westchester County and its dozens of upscale nurseries and garden centers.

From mom-and-pop operations to large tropical greenhouses filled with exotic trees and ferns to run-down nurseries that looked pathetic but often had something wonderful on a far bench—the result always seemed to be a van filled to capacity with unusual flowering plants to cut from or to sell.

Summer was a breeze, the scores of nurseries scattered nearby brimming with endless stretches of perennials, garden roses, and flowering shrubs. And once we had unearthed enough hothouses in the surrounding countryside to secure an ample supply of geraniums, citrus trees, begonias, and other warm-weather delights, winter fell into place as well.

The Bridge family, located just north of Greenwich, Connecticut—three brothers and a sister and Mom and Dad—ran a savvy little operation. They experimented with growing flowers we knew from the fresh-flower market but had never seen growing in clay pots—*Euphorbia fulgens*, gloriosa lilies, Eucharist lilies, and others.

In their plastic houses out back, past the scruffy little water garden filled with papyrus and floating water hyacinths, they stashed an abundant supply of herbs and geraniums of all sorts, many of them ancient stock plants from which they took their cuttings, so these were characterful and perfect for magazine photo shoots when the plants had to be sizable and look great, even way out of season. Along with quince and the usual flowering trees, they forced bridal-wreath and other spireas, redbud, and pear blossoms. It was here that we first started our practice of sifting through a nursery's pile of discarded clay pots to find odd shapes or discolored, mossy, or weathered ones.

Nearby at Sprainbrook, a nursery renowned for its African violets, strepto-carpus, and sinningias, benches loaded with pots of Rieger begonias—full, beautiful shapes, crowned with gorgeous flowers and perfect, plump foliage—regularly supplied our table centerpieces with material. Sprainbrook had the

PREVIOUS PAGES: Be inventive. Matching these playful little narcissus to a shallow clay saucer makes a delightfully fresh presentation. Whenever possible, assemble as much variety as you can get your hands on.

bright idea of growing the miniature spring bulbs suchs as grape hyacinth, 'Tête-à-Tête' narcissus, chionodoxa, and *Scilla siberica* in shallow clay saucers rather than the sometimes cumbersome-looking larger clay pots.

Completing this trio of suppliers was Rudy Nabel's nursery in nearby White Plains, New York, always filled with an ample supply of bougainvillea, jasmines, hibiscus, and a wealth of citrus trees—tangerine, lime, ponderosa lemon, and Seville and calamondin oranges. At times, when the fruit became too heavy and threatened to snap a limb, Rudy would offer us a pair of clippers and we would have a great branch for a special arrangement. At other times, we would simply buy the plant itself and use it all.

Summertime at Nabel's was crowned with majestic geraniums: tall, thick columns and tree-form standards of every color from deepest magenta to the most vivid orange, and endless rows of hanging baskets of the cascading "balcony" strains one encounters all over Europe in lipstick colors of hot pink, coral, and bright vermilion, all perfect for cutting. Growing alongside tree-form lantanas (the pale lavender one was especially soft and pendant, with cascades of tiny flowers) were enormous chalk-blue plumbagos, five-foot-tall dierna begonias, and huge pink-trumpeted mandevilla vines.

Meadowbrook Farms, a beautiful Pennsylvania estate with notable gardens and a productive range of greenhouses owned by Liddon Pennock (a venerable name in the flower business), supplied us with hanging baskets stuffed with vivid nasturtiums, intriguing climbing ferns grown on forked branches, weathered produce boxes of primroses and English daisies, and lovely jasmine plants, both white and dazzling yellow, as well as stacks of mossy pots.

One of the wildest places I visited on this route was Ott's Exotic Plants outside the little Pennsylvania town of Schwenksville. This immense glass structure, reminiscent of the Crystal Palace but plunked down in the middle of nowhere, has a wealth of great, sometimes bizarre offerings: polypodium and hart's-tongue ferns, alocasias and odd anthuriums, allamanda, calliandra, and rows and rows of rangy-but-interesting succulents. The really crazy pieces were often down at the end of the farthest glasshouse, chained off behind a sign that read "Not for Sale—Employees Only." I almost always found something incredible along that forbidden path—some strange begonia I'd never

Don't overlook any cutting opportunities—even really exotic material like the deadly nightshade shown here can work in an arrangement.

Search for the best spots
to put your flower choices.
The brilliant jewel tones
of these nasturtiums,
ABOVE, show their true
colors when properly lit.
LEFT: Clematis vines, each
unique in form and color
and set in clay pots, make
natural table centerpieces
in the rotunda of the
National Gallery of Art.

seen before, a shallow wooden flat of sedum cuttings all tangled together and looking like a little desert landscape, a huge crown-of-thorns trained into a globe, a gnarled old fruit tree in a great Italian pot, or rows of flowering jade trees six feet tall.

On my way back to New York, I always stopped at a charming family-owned operation called The Rhoads Garden. It was the Rhoads boys who produced, far out of their season, the extraordinary clematis plants that ultimately graced the tables of Paul Mellon's retirement dinner in Washington, D.C., a few years back.

These were but a few of the places I would drive to in search of unusual plants and flowers. Others came to us.

Holland Acres is a story in itself. For years a supplier of beautiful locally grown cut tulips to the New York market, Holland Acres started the "wood flat" phenomenon. For reasons of convenience and handling, Holland Acres grew their cutting tulips in natural wood crates, or flats, each holding eighty or more bulbs. Once planted, the flats had to be chilled for a number of weeks. For economy of space they were stacked as high as could be in "chilling" houses; then, as they were needed, the boxes were brought into warmer greenhouses for gradual forcing. It's a little unclear who first saw these boxes of tulips growing and imagined that they might make wonderful objects in and of themselves, but whoever it was did, and the phenomenon was born. Nowadays, every conceivable bulb—from lily-of-the-valley pips to fritillaria—is grown for sale in a wooden box, and these boxes come in more affordable and more convenient quarter- and half-flat sizes. They're even available by mail through catalogs such as Smith & Hawken.

One day we found Heidi, or she found us, and from that moment she has mined her sources in the woods and gardens of upper New Jersey for us, cutting and bringing in the widest array of plant material imaginable. Spring and summer yield apple, pear, crab, magnolia, quince, and euonymus, all laden with emerging flowers. In fall and winter she harvests fruited branches of all sorts, from dark blue-black privet berries to the tiniest yellow crabapples. During the winter months, Heidi cuts varieties of holly and other evergreens not found in the more traditional flower shops.

Spring flowers help dispel winter's gloom—a half-flat of pink pencil tulips makes an instant spring garden in a city living room window.

The flowers and trees on the following list are placed in the month when they are at their peak. Temperature, latitude, geographical area, and general overall weather conditions will dictate deviations (plus or minus about three weeks). Most wildflowers and woody stems *cannot* be used in floral foam.

The last column lists whether it is *wild* (W), *cultivated* (C), a *flower* (F), or a *berry, fruit, or seed* (BFS).

FEBRUARY

birch (gray, yellow, white) W-C-BFS

curly willow C-F

maple (red, sugar, Norway, Japanese)
 W-C-F-BFS

pussy willow W-C-F

skunk cabbage W-F

MARCH

cornelian cherry C-F

forsythia C-F

Korean azalea C-F

peach C-F

P.J.M. rhododendron C-F

plum C-F

quince C-F

star magnolia C-F

weeping willow W-C-F

witch hazel W-C-F-BFS

APRIL

andromeda W-C-F

apple, crabapple W-C-F

cherry (Kwanzan, Japanese weeping, sweet,
 sour) W-C-F

dogwood W-C-F

magnolia C-F

pear (bosc, bradford, pyrus) C-F

plum C-F

violet W-C-F

winter cress W-F

Don't hesitate to cut from flowering plants. This box of narcissus hardly missed the dozen we cut for the table.

MAY

azalea W-C-F

bridal wreath spirea C-F

columbine W-C-F

euphorbia W-C-F

honeysuckle (bush, vine) W-C-F

iris (Siberian, bearded, wild) W-C-F

lilac C-F

lily of the valley C-F

Paul's scarlet hawthorn C-F

peonies C-F

poppy C-F

redbud / Judas tree W-C-F

rhododendron C-F

vibernum (doublefile, opulus) C-F

wild roses W-C-F

wisteria C-F

JUNE

beard tongue W-F

beauty bush C-F

black-eyed Susan W-C-F

Carolina spice bush C-F

clover W-C-F

common buttercup W-F

crown vetch W-C-F-BFS

coreopsis W-C-F

currant C-BFS

deutzia C-F

dock W-F

enkianthus C-F

foxglove W-C-F

kousa dogwood C-F

meadowsweet W-F

mock orange C-F

moth mullein W-F-BFS

mountain laurel W-C-F

Queen-Anne's-lace W-F

rose campion C-F

roses W-C-F

thistle W-F

vipers bugloss W-F

weigelia C-F

wild sweet pea W-C-F-BFS

yarrow W-C-F

yucca W-C-F

JULY

- ailanthus / tree of heaven W-C-BFS
- bee balm / bergamot W-C-F
- black raspberry W-C-BFS
- blue vervane W-F
- bouncing bet W-F
- bur cucumber W-BFS
- bur reed W-BFS
- butter and eggs W-F
- butterfly weed / railroad Annie W-C-F
- cattail / punk W-BFS
- fleabane W-F
- goldenrod / solidago W-C-F
- grasses W-C-BFS
- hydrangea (Annabelle Lee, Nikko) C-F
- Joe Pye weed W-F
- loostrife / lithrum W-C-F
- meadow rue W-F
- mint W-C-F
- mountain ash C-BFS
- phlox C-F
- queen of the prairie W-C-F
- smoketree C-BFS
- steeplebush W-F
- sumac (Winged, Smooth, Staghorn)
  W-C-BFS
- sweet pepperbush W-C-F

AUGUST

- aster W-C-F
- autumn joy C-F
- bayberry W-C-BFS
- blue spirea C-F
- boneset W-F
- butterfly bush C-F
- catalpa W-C-BFS
- common mullein W-F
- crabapple W-C-BFS
- devil's walking stick W-BFS
- horse tail reed W
- ironweed W-F
- jewel weed / touch-me-not W-F
- live forever W-F
- obedient plant C-F
- peach C-BFS
- pear W-C-BFS
- pearly everlasting W-F
- pokeweed W-F-BFS
- Saint Johnswort W-C-F
- sneezeweed W-C-F
- swamp rose mallow W-C-F
- teasel W-F

SEPTEMBER

- bittersweet vine W-C-BFS
- grapes W-C-BFS

- hydrangea (Pee Gee, Lace) C-F
- milkweed W-BFS
- nannyberry W-C-BFS
- porcelain berry W-BFS
- rose hips W-C-BFS
- Russian olive W-C-BFS
- wild clematis W-C-F

OCTOBER

- American bamboo W-C-BFS
- doll's eyes W-BFS
- eastern burning bush C-BFS
- euonymus (Cork Bark, Winged)
  W-C-BFS
- firethorn C-BFS
- hawthorn C-BFS
- privet W-C-BFS

NOVEMBER

- dogwood (Yellow twig, Red twig) W-C
- winterberry W-C-BFS
- witch hazel W-C-BFS

DECEMBER

- evergreens (Pine, Juniper, Hemlock,
  Spruce, Cedar) W-C
- holly W-C-BFS

Little by little a momentum for new kinds of flowers began to be established, and especially once the shelter magazines started to feature casual arrangements of real garden flowers, the marketplace followed suit.

Our task was made much easier when suppliers from outlying areas began to bring their flowers into the city. A few Westchester gardeners would load up their station wagons with cosmos, coreopsis, hollyhocks, bearded irises, and any other varieties that could withstand the rigors of travel. Nurserymen learned to sell excess crops to the city markets, and perennials grown for far-flung gardens often found themselves gracing New York tables instead.

The city's wholesale market gradually responded to this new direction, and for a number of years now, alongside the vendors who supply the old familiars to the less adventurous are sellers who offer a seemingly endless assortment of new flower choices.

Variety, variety, and more variety. A handful of exquisite roses is worth boxes of the more common varieties.

Sifting through the Flower Choices

WE BUY ONLY FLOWERS WE LIKE. Since we felt from our first days on Madison Avenue that the flowers we stocked and sent should offer the possibility of surprising and delighting the recipients whenever possible, we learned to vary what we bought, even from week to week, and continually looked for flowers that were not so commonly used. Each time we went to the market, we tried to look for a full range of colors, shapes, sizes, and textures that would give us the maximum set of possibilities for the day's work.

We have always steered clear of the whole range of inexpensive flowers found on every street corner, as well as certain overused or overexposed varieties (two examples as I write this are rubrum lilies and French tulips). We still believe that every flower needs a rest now and then. We tire of using the same materials over and over and look to an ever-changing mix to keep our work fresh. Certain flowers—'Sterling Silver' roses and 'Casablanca' lilies, for instance—have recently had the misfortune to become "signature" flowers on the New York scene and thus, through no inherent fault of their own, have lost their cachet, at least for us. When anything becomes *de rigueur*, we often pass it by, at least for a time.

We quickly learned which flowers combine easily with others and which resist combination and stand too clearly on their own. From the very beginning, the brash tropical flowers didn't appeal to us. While we frequently work with softer tropical materials—cuttings of chalky-blue plumbago flowers, gloriosa lilies, jasmine branches, clouds of fuzzy yellow mimosa—the strong shapes, large scale, and often garish colors of gingers, anthuriums, orchid sprays, birds-of-paradise, proteas, and the like—as exciting as they may be for some—simply held nothing for us.

Leafing through this book will give you a very good idea of the flowers we love. Some of our favorites include columbines, fritillarias (from the tiny pale-purple checkerboard lilies to the giant orange-flowered imperialis—even though they smell skunky), all of the miniature bulbs (such as single and double grape hyacinths and species tulips), Siberian and bearded irises, lavender, trumpet lilies (such as 'Black Dragon' and 'African Queen'), peonies, all sorts

BELOW: *Liliane François stands in front of her lovely Paris shop showing off a bundle of garden irises just dropped off by an amateur grower.*
OPPOSITE: *Rose cuttings from our country garden—a motley mix to be sure—include a tiny-flowered old-fashioned rugosa hybrid.*

[*Some of the Roses Billy Buys*]

DUTCH

'*Eveline*'—a small delicate spray
rose, pale bubble-gum pink

'*Matador*'—brilliant reddish orange
tulip-shaped rose with lots of petals

'*Nicole*'—a spectacular bicolor, dark
red inside and silvery gray outside

'*Paso Doble*'—a lipstick-pink version
of 'Nicole'

'*Vicky Brown*'—a smaller bicolor, orange and cream

CALIFORNIA

'*Abraham Darby*'—a superb
branched rose with exquisite creamy
blush shadings

'*Brandy*'—deep pumpkin tinged
with red

'*Bredonne*'—old-fashioned-looking,
smallish, pale pink

'*English Garden*'—a full, flat, dahlia-
shaped flower in pale cream shades

'*Fair Bianca*'—color nuances
from pale ivory to burnt cream with
a red blush and a unique myrrhlike fragrance

'*Mr. Lincoln*'—a huge flower head,
dark, almost black-red and wildly
fragrant

'*Playboy*'—a vivid orange that shades
from yellow to a burnt vermilion

'*Sheer Bliss*'—hydroponically grown,
with enormous blowsy pink flowers

FRENCH

'*Anna*'—extremely reliable and long-
lived, ivory blush to pink

'*Josepha*'—an unusual brownish rose
that seldom opens; looks somewhat
like a big fat pinecone

'*Madame Pompadour*'—big and fat in
pink-orange red

'*Marella*'—fragrant, blowsy, and
yellow with sunburnt edges

NOTHING is more important than an abundant and inspired selection of flowers from which to choose.

Always leave plenty of space for natural flowers to strut their stuff. While identical flowers such as the checkerboard lilies and grape hyacinths, ABOVE LEFT, can look good just jammed into a jar, mixes of dissimilar flowers need plenty of breathing room to flaunt their wares properly. ABOVE: In good light, tulips develop and elongate. Give them space to grow. LEFT: The sexy, sinuous shapes of tiny leucocorenes writhes about in a Phillipe Starck vase. OPPOSITE: Tiny delights culled from our spring country garden include trout lilies, actea narcissus, leucojum, leggy forsythia, and emerging catkins from our weeping willow tree.

[*Flowers We Steer Clear Of*]

asters—the little roadside varieties look like cheap filler—pretty in a field but a liability in a mix; the larger pink and purple flowers are too stiff and chunky.

baby's-breath—the most *overused* flower of all, and misused, we feel, to "lighten up" other flowers.

bells-of-Ireland—a strong shape and a washed-out shade of green that's hard to combine with other flowers.

carnations—much too commonly used; the colors are flat and unappealing (don't even look at the dyed ones), though occasionally we buy one of the French fringed varieties.

chrysanthemums—much, much too commonly used and often appear in flat, unappealing colors such as washed-out yellow and pale grayish purple.

daisies—perfectly nice but *burdened* by our awareness of their cheapness.

Easter lilies—too associative.

florist's irises—the garden varieties have more-delicate shadings and markings and a wide range of colors—including some bizarre shades of gray and brown.

florist's pussy willow—too straight, too much like a dried flower, and far too common.

forsythia—there's a lemony green to its yellowness that we find unappealing, although occasionally forsythia is useful if it is long and leggy; grown as a short straight stem it's awful and useless.

gerbera daisies—as amazing as these flowers are, especially given their astonishing range of colors, they often look dyed or fake to our eyes; they stand out rather than blend in.

of poppies, nasturtiums, clematis, geraniums of all kinds, Christmas rose, perfectly grown single tuberoses, rhododendron and azalea flowers, scabiosa, bridal-wreath, lots of kinds of tulips, real and hybrid lilacs, and flowering and berried branches of all sorts. **AN INSPIRED SELECTION OF RAW MATERIALS VIRTUALLY GUARANTEES SUCCESSFUL RESULTS**, while an uninspired selection leads only to mediocrity. Remember, in natural flower arranging, no other decision in the arranging process comes even close to the importance of inspired flower choices.

Stocking the Shelves

When it came to containers, for us, the floral-supply houses didn't cut it. In the first place, we were looking for the simplest shapes in clear glass, and much of what was being sold in the market was either cut, colored, etched, frosted, opalescent, or oddly shaped. The colors and surfaces of the solid containers were unappealing to us: fashionable "berry" colors or sleek and shiny black and chrome.

Second, so much of what was being sold was so inexpensive that we felt it ended up just looking cheap. This price business raises a complex issue, and to a certain extent, it's not only the fault of the suppliers. Flower arranging has been so undervalued for so long that it can't very often sustain accessories of other than the most minimal value, although that doesn't mean that the ones offered have to be gaudy or unattractive.

Of course, we're the ones who've made flower arrangements in a lettuce crate, a film can, an Alka-Seltzer bottle, a Thunderbird wine bottle, and a waste basket, so it might be asked, "Who are we to judge others' choices?"

In any event, after a search of the gift market and other traditional sources, we came to the conclusion that much of what is specifically designed for florists to use is self-consciously fashionable or trendy, not simple and straightforward, and so, as we did with cut flowers and flowering plants, we directed our search for containers to other places.

We found our first simple glass containers in Libby Glass's food-storage line—a ginger jar available in several sizes and a slightly irregular cylinder called a "barber pole"—both meant to be used as kitchen canisters (we simply discarded the lids). Even though they were very inexpensive, they didn't *look* cheap to us. Perhaps this was because the shapes were classic. Cream-colored pottery pickle crocks—also destined for the pantry—were useful for more casual mixes. The only simple glass vase sold in floral-supply houses at that time was the globe, or "goldfish bowl," which we found difficult to work with, both because it was hard to get the initial stems to stay where they were put (the globe form has no bottom edges to catch and hold a stem or branch) and because the roundness of the flower mix seemed to mimic the shape of the container below.

Eventually some market-supply houses added these simple glass shapes to their shelves. Due to the ease with which they hold flowers, these containers dominated most of our work for several years. Then as these shapes became more popular, we switched to even simpler cylinders and rectangles.

An early search of commercial restaurant-supply stores turned up inexpensive barware such as "zombies"—tall, thin glasses—as well as standard highball and old-fashioned sizes. For many years, we raided medical-supply houses for interesting laboratory items—beakers, flasks, and glass dishes of various sorts. Today we are returning more and more to inexpensive tableware for our everyday containers. We use ribbed French jelly jars and crudely made pale-green drinking glasses from Mexico and Portugal for simple, casual flower

WITH THE RISE of numerous inexpensive home-furnishings stores such as Ikea, Crate & Barrel, and the Pottery Barn, a wide selection of inexpensive glassware is becoming more and more available to amateur and professional alike. Don't overlook these potential container sources.

liatris—we don't much like the electric color and we hate the flower's perfect straightness; it often seems to blast out of arrangements.

Peruvian lilies—although the individual flowers can be beautiful, since they are so uniform we find them stiff and predictable in a mix.

production gladiolas—gladiolas produced as straight stems are too stiff; no matter how you try to use them, they radiate out of an arrangement rather than blend in.

snapdragons—unless we can tuck them well into a mix, we usually pass them by, feeling that they are thought of as being inexpensive or cheap; but, since they are often grown on very long stems, we occasionally use the intensely colored ones for our big arrangements.

statice—dry and fake-looking and associated with dried-flower arrangements.

strawflower—dull-colored and too much like a dried flower.

tiger lilies—acid-orange Asiatic (upright) lilies, coupled with an equally sharp lemon-yellow counterpart, are overused and difficult to blend with softer-colored flowers.

yarrow—too much like a dried flower; the colors are dead and unappealing.

A simple pilsner glass holds two lovely tulips perfectly. What more do you need?

mixes, and an intriguing new set of shapes—hand-blown in Egypt—for our more adventurous offerings. One glass is slant-sided, but narrower at the top than the bottom—the reverse of the usual flared glass; a footed goblet sports a shapely profile; a traditional pilsner shape, although it holds little water and needs refreshing often, holds a wide range of simple flowers perfectly. And on occasion, when a gift calls for a very special presentation, we turn to our elegant line of Viennese glassware—from the famed shop Lobmeyr—and fashion a striking mix in their exquisite champagne flute.

Finally, whereas elaborate containers might look out of place in their eventual home, simple glass shapes are suitable for a variety of settings, from traditional to more relaxed country rooms and to every kind of modern decor.

Over the years, numerous potters have fashioned simple shapes for us in a

MANY FLORISTS solve the globe problem by using chickenwire, clear glass marbles, crinkled iridescent cellophane, or river pebbles to hold the flowers in place. We believe that a container should be capable of holding flowers without the arranger having to resort to extraneous devices.

LEFT: *Just-gathered narcissus casually stuffed into a drinking glass help dress down an elegant interior.*
BELOW: *At times, one perfect something is plenty. A Martha Washington geranium cutting sits on one edge of our ink-blue handle pot.*

[*Our Current Inventory of All-purpose Containers*]

clear glass rectangles (all sizes are nominal):

1×5×5; 1×3×5 (Sugahara, Japan—wholesale
and retail call 415-563-3100)

5×7×16; 5×10×10 (wholesale only—for nearest
supplier call Brody Corporation 800-362-7639)

3×5×11; 2×3×9 (wholesale only—for nearest
supplier call Crisa Corporation 800-643-9093)

10×4×3; 8×7×4; 7×4×3; 6×4×3
(Colony Glass 800-543-0357)

clear glass ginger jar and urn shapes (wholesale
floral supply houses and various manufacturers;
N.K. Florist Supplies 201-784-1007)

low cylindrical "salad bowls" (Crisa Corporation)

clear glass cylinders (through wholesale floral
supply houses and various manufacturers;
N.K. Florist Supplies)

12" oval (wholesale only; Crisa Corporation)

drinking glasses: hand-blown Egyptian tableware
from Vetra; shapes: Pilsner; Sphinx L-footed
goblet; Pyramid L-slant-sided drinking glass;
Tumbler

French jelly jars (available in most housewares
stores—from Arcoroc)

These are all available at retail from Pure
Mädderlake.

range of carefully chosen soft glazes. A slant-sided vase mimicking a clay flowerpot without the heavy rim, finished in warm dove gray, pale robin's-egg
blue, or a watery celadon shade of gray-green, holds a bunch of tulips to perfection. A collection of hand-shaped jars with tiny handles—glazed in a soft,
matte finish of deep ink blue—is perfect for a single flower or two, or discards
from larger arrangements. Our cherub pot—a small cup ringed with dancing
putti, which we make in an ivory glaze as well as natural terra cotta—is a big
seller, especially around the holidays. A perfect and inexpensive little gift filled
with violets or other tiny flowers, it's also useful for holding a votive candle or
as a cachepot for tiny plants such as miniature roses, small cyclamens, or can-
dy-colored primroses.

We seldom use baskets, for a variety of reasons. Every now and then we
come across a rustic or rugged basket we like, but for the most part we find a
certain amount of associative baggage attending flowers arranged in baskets.
Perhaps because baskets have been a traditional favorite with many florists
over the years, they seem to have a too-familiar, commercial aura about them.
Since we strive to find our own look, we try to avoid associative elements.
Also, while inexpensive glassware is often perfectly presentable-looking—if at
times somewhat ordinary—more often than not, inexpensive baskets simply
look cheap. As most of our flower orders can't support an expensive container, for economic reasons alone baskets would be out of the question.

When it comes to containers, even the sky's not the limit. The tiny Tabasco bottle—saved from a bloody Mary served someplace between New York and Amsterdam—holds a toad lily flower to perfection; pure white thalia daffodils crowd a battered green pail; New Zealand peonies, flown up in the middle of our winter, nestle in a wine crate, ready for delivery; tiny grape hyacinths pop out of an old redware pot; and a shapely container mimics its shapely tulip occupants.

Pure Mädderlake has always reserved a few shelves for a diverse selection of flea-market bargains, from redware crocks, painted tin pails, and old glass battery jars to some of the wildest shapes the Ohio potteries ever produced. And one shelf in the store still holds such street finds as the galvanized film canister offered to us by our garbagemen on 73rd Street who had noticed our penchant for strange containers in our window displays. This large hexagonal metal can ended up, its hinged lid askew and filled with tumbling flowers, center stage on a pedestal for the opening of the Lincoln Center Film Archives. A host of wooden packing boxes and wine crates, brightly labeled produce containers, bottles and cans—"attractive" discards of all sorts—rounds out our collection.

From the very first days of the shop in the Village, we've searched for interesting clay pots to help make both green and flowering plants look special. Combing religiously through the debris under nursery benches and sifting through the discards out back at every garden center I stopped at, I found unusual shapes as well as pots covered with the patina of time and season.

We were among the first to champion the use of mossy pots in fine settings: the marriage of plant to pot is more natural-looking and the result more comfortable and timeless, not freshly done or self-conscious. We still feel that different kinds of pots should be mixed together, that saucers and pots should *not* be perfectly matched, and that pots should not look oversized for what they contain. It's maddening to look at a room full of flowering plants, each carefully placed in an identical, oversized, brand-new pot and saucer, all lined up looking as uncomfortable as fresh recruits in an army. Plants used in settings should look as if they *belong* to the room and should reflect the fact that they each may have come from different seasons and moments, not appear to be a rush order from a local grower.

Among the most beautiful and sensual clay pots in the world are English orchid pots, which are now hard to find and expensive when found. Wanting an ample supply for ourselves, and feeling that the time had come to introduce clay pots with more personality to a wider audience, we started to make our own pots at a price people could afford. They approximate the qualities we find so charming in the English pots: slightly irregular shapes, textures, and coloring. Once we had figured out a method for making them, we began to consider how to add some element of decoration that wouldn't look cute or forced. So as each pot in our new Number Pot line is unmolded, our potter presses a stamp into the wet clay, changing the number each time so that no two will ever be alike.

Why must all clay pots be alike? Each of these Number Pots looks and feels unique and lends its special character to what's placed in it. Work with different container shapes and proportions to make plants look special and individual.

A soft-colored mix of oleander, roses, and geraniums is held in place by branched stems of blue sage in an old pitcher.

Finding a Voice

In the beginning, it was extremely difficult to make ourselves understood. Since we were evolving a style and an approach to making and using flowers that was different from many other flower shops, we didn't know quite how to express ourselves except by example. That did little good for potential customers who had never seen our work.

We began to examine how other shops traditionally communicated with each other and with their customers, and we concluded that the issue of intelligent and effective communication is troublesome.

The problem, of course, is that due to a lack of common ground between florists and their clients, both parties are hampered by a mutual inability to express or convey what results they desire. The customary means for bridging that gap is to create "models" to be photographed and then chosen by a customer. Since the flowers have already been designed and captured in an im-

---

[*To Place a Telephone Order with an Unknown Florist*]

Unless you know the style and quality of a florist's work, it might be wiser to ask for something simpler than a mixed arrangement. Begin by asking what flowers the florist himself would choose from the day's offerings, or what he feels is especially pretty or different in his shop. If you're lucky, you will be engaged by his reply and you can feel confident that a beautiful gift will ensue. If his response is a usual string of flower choices—long-stemmed red roses, gerbera daisies, blue irises, carnations, or freesias—you'll have to do some fast thinking. Press for more off-beat choices. If none are forthcoming, choose the least problematic offering and then ask more about it: size, color, condition of the flowers. Unless you sense some real enthusiasm, move on to something else. Once you have made a choice, describe the manner in which you want the gift to be assembled and presented. Try to visualize what they will be sending. Don't be afraid to ask

questions and work through his answers until you're sure that you're sending something that pleases you. A good florist will try to help you fashion what *you* want—be patient, but be specific and be clear.

From the list above, for example, if we had been assured that they were full, plump, and shapely, we might have chosen the freesias. We would then have asked for them to be loosely arranged in a simply shaped clear glass vase, accompanied by a plain white envelope and card, and wrapped in plain tissue—no trailing ribbons or decorated wrapping paper. Be careful of the word "arranged," though; some florists see arranging as an "artistic" endeavor and end up with something decidedly unnatural. In this case, the better word might be "assembled," or even "put." Stress that you want it to look casual and natural.

On occasions when a florist doesn't have a plain glass container, ask if the flowers could

be water-tubed and either wrapped in clear cellophane or plain tissue, or sent in a plain white rose box. Tell him *not* to add extraneous greens, and make sure that your selection has not been wired or otherwise manipulated.

Should no flower choices appeal, ask about potted orchids or flowering plants. Specify a plain clay pot, as small as possible. Some florists, eager to be horticulturally correct and provide plenty of room for the future roots to develop, choose pots that ludicrously dwarf their contents. Have the florist enclose a small glass plate or a simple terra-cotta saucer. Insist that he use no colored foil, cheap ribbon, or other trappings. We prefer used, mossy pots that make the occupant look much more comfortable than do spanking new ones, but that's probably a tall order in most places.

Don't be afraid to ask questions and work through the answers until you're sure that you're sending something that pleases you.

age, this image can be passed to other florists who can re-create the exact same thing on command. While this method most certainly solves the communication problem, and makes for safe and easy commerce, for us it raises a number of disturbing issues.

First, it reduces the creative act to the re-creation of a preconceived product. Second, it dictates that a uniform cadre of flowers be available throughout the country (or the world for that matter) for the models to be replicated properly. Therefore, an arrangement ordered in San Francisco will be the same arrangement as one made in Miami Beach or Boston or New Orleans or Rome. The net result of this system is the worldwide production of a narrow band of cut-flower choices in a field that should have virtually limitless offerings, for in truth, each place has its own set of unique capabilities, local resources, and talented designers.

We reasoned that there must be another way of communicating so that the possibilities would not be so uniform and limited. Our answer to the problem of communicating was twofold.

First, we sought to start with simple descriptive language that would gradually lead to a desired result, using general, nonproduct words in the beginning and becoming more specific only later on. For instance, to describe an imagined flower arrangement, we might use such words as gardenlike, woodsy, loose and airy, French or Dutch or English, like a nosegay, elegant and stylish, sexy, childlike, summery, autumnal, wintry. Each of these initial images might suggest certain kinds of flowers and ways of assembling them. These could be further described with modifying or qualifying words, such as grand, simple, full-blown, tiny, precious, sweet, colorful, cheery, quiet.

Working in this manner, we begin with a clean idea—not a preconceived "model"—that might lead to something interesting and individual. For example, when someone calls to send a gift, we often begin by asking what reaction the gift is meant to provoke or what purpose it is to serve. Is it meant to overwhelm someone with congratulations? Send a quiet token of thanks? Celebrate a simple moment, such as the arrival of spring? Fill in for spring in the midst of winter's doldrums? Express sadness over a loss? Each motive suggests a radically different way of choosing and assembling the flowers.

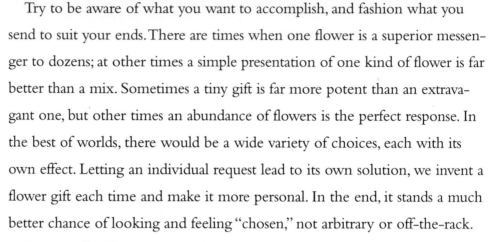

There's no need to settle for cheap mass-produced ribbons. Look at this selection of inexpensive remnants from a local trimmings store.

LEARN TO MAKE your gifts look personal. For a friend, Billy lodged two very strange plants into a wooden box turned on end, then added a postcard—handmade on our copy machine—wrapped it all in clear cellophane, with some ribbon to secure a card.

Try to be aware of what you want to accomplish, and fashion what you send to suit your ends. There are times when one flower is a superior messenger to dozens; at other times a simple presentation of one kind of flower is far better than a mix. Sometimes a tiny gift is far more potent than an extravagant one, but other times an abundance of flowers is the perfect response. In the best of worlds, there would be a wide variety of choices, each with its own effect. Letting an individual request lead to its own solution, we invent a flower gift each time and make it more personal. In the end, it stands a much better chance of looking and feeling "chosen," not arbitrary or off-the-rack.

For a small offering, you might send a tiny crock or pot of little violas (Johnny-jump-ups), or a farmstand mushroom basket filled with pansies, or a little square container of sweet Williams or fragrant yellow narcissus. Certain kinds of flower gifts should be lighthearted and not overdone.

At the other end of the spectrum is the extravagant, congratulatory gift, which suggests something sizable and impressive, bold and expensive—maybe a full box of brightly colored 'Gudoschnik' tulips; an armload of garden roses all done up in clear cellophane and elegant grosgrain ribbons; a bright and sizzling mix of brilliantly colored poppies, deep blue and purple delphiniums, double cherry branches, and dark pink calla lilies, all nestled in a wooden box of excelsior.

Flowers whose purpose is to express sadness and loss must be the most carefully chosen of all, for they will speak of things for which we cannot find the words. In this case, those that gently touch rather than overwhelm may be the most appropriate message bearers. Since the most intensely communicative flowers are often the smallest—like rare perfumes, they are concentrations of the loveliest bits nature has to offer—to convey a sense of loss and sadness we might choose to make a small, quiet bouquet of flowers, simply and deftly combined, and very quietly wrapped and presented.

Make mental notes of the kinds of flowers you find appealing as you encounter them in books, magazines, gardens, and stores, and try to be specific in your future requests. **A LIST OF SIMPLE WORDS AND IDEAS YOU HAVE IN COMMON WITH YOUR FLORIST WILL ALMOST GUARANTEE BETTER FUTURE RESULTS.**

The second way to communicate ideas is to find and describe an image or an event—maybe even produce a picture—that sums up the desired result without being a specific product to replicate. Just a few well-turned phrases or a handful of perfect words can provide us with everything we need in order to imagine the whole setting and all its various parts. For example, a wedding described as an all-stops-pulled-out royal affair suggests exactly how to begin imagining and talking about the particulars and provides a yardstick against which all the various ideas and decisions can be measured. Choices in all categories would be lavish, dramatic, and elegant even to the point of exaggeration. Flowers would be showy, expensive-looking, and stylish—giant Aureatum and deep burgundy trumpet lilies, extra-long-stemmed roses in ivory or royal red—not simple, homespun, and gardeny. The bouquets would be tailored and overscaled. Loads of candles, garlands and bowers of flowers, a host of trumpets—each choice destined to blend into one grand setting.

At our first meeting with a wedding client a few years ago, we were shown a picture clipped from a magazine: a simple weathered iron arbor covered with pale pink roses, quietly arched over the center pathway of a garden somewhere in France. This single romantic image summed up the whole idea of what the wedding should look and *feel* like, and it served as the sole, but extremely informative, piece of information that ultimately led us to the simple and elegant setting we created.

Here's another example of how this process can work. In late 1991, Calvin Klein asked me to make flowers for the introduction of his new women's line

[*Wrapping a Gift of Flowers*]

The first glimpse a recipient has of a gift of flowers is the package. The same care that governs the choice of flowers should extend to the package as well.

In cold weather, we always wrap our flowers in clear cellophane so that the flowers, though protected from the cold, are still the show. We use a plain cardboard box and plenty of kraft-colored tissue to cushion and secure the vase. In fact, since the packing boxes we buy are white outside and brown inside, we assemble them inside out to get our look. We reject most commercial ribbons as looking too cheap and synthetic, and comb through the shelves and drawers of trimmings stores for inexpensive and expensive alternatives. Every city and town has sources for great ribbons—there's no good excuse to stock the cheap paper and shiny acetate ones. For our signature ribbon, we print our name on simple colors of one-inch cotton webbing.

We keep a supply of small manila cards and envelopes on hand (found in an office-supply store), or add hand-chosen postcards fastened to the package by a simple cord threaded through a hole punched in the corner of the card. In addition to currently available postcards, we search flea-market vendors regularly for inexpensive old flower cards. A card is a great place to add a little whimsy to a gift. Search about for the ones that appeal to you.

The tea-colored garden roses used to introduce a recent Calvin Klein summer collection grace the showroom for days after the show.

for summer. Rather than using the globes filled with elegant white calla lilies that so often accompany his couture collections, he felt that this time the show flowers should reflect the idea of the collection.

The colors and even some of the character of his new collection had partly evolved from a few pages in Irving Penn's book *Flowers*. The most explicit image was of two or three single roses in faded shades of dusty pink and pale grays and browns, both firm and fallen. Well, this picture was not just about colors or specific flowers. It was about passing time and a sense of ease and comfort, and so I set out to capture all of these qualities in the flowers.

I called the various nurseries and found that, even though it was late October, Nabel's Nursery had not yet cut back all of their roses. Rudy Nabel was able to set aside a dozen or so pots that still had long, arching branches of foliage—fading fruit and flowers and natural-looking leaves.

The soft colors that Calvin had used for his dresses were to be found in the old English roses being grown in California. I needed big and spectacular flowers, so my New York supplier, Dutch Flower Line, asked their source to cut 'Fair Bianca', 'Bredonne', 'English Garden', and 'Abraham Darby', each as long as the cutters could possibly stand without damaging the plant, giving

[*When Grand Is Good/When Smaller Is Better*]

Most people worry that the flowers they're sending will not be big enough or impressive enough, but in truth, the size of the offering is hardly the proper measure. Worry instead that the *choice* of flowers sent will not convey the special feelings you intend.

A gift of flowers should represent the sender's intended sentiment in an appropriate way, and an overscaled gift can be exactly the *wrong* thing. Although there may be times when you may wish to overwhelm a recipient, more often than not a perfect little choice stands a better chance of delighting and surprising. First, it's clear that it's quality not quantity you have chosen, and it shows that you're confident in your choice. Second, unless the setting itself

can accommodate it, a large mix can simply look awkward and out of place. Third, many people are uncomfortable if they think that a huge amount of money has been spent on what they get (there are, of course, notable exceptions to this), but a small yet perfectly delightful offering is easy to receive. Fourth, and of course this depends on what the flowers look like, large mixes can remind us of special occasions (weddings and funerals, for example) and thereby convey the wrong message.

A thank-you gift for a dinner party is best sent the day after, but if you want to send flowers before, keep them small. Many hosts will have planned all of their flowers, so a sizable gift the day of the party is hard to deal with.

Particularly in places such as hospital rooms, where space is very limited, smaller gifts of flowers are far more welcome. Choose especially carefully here, for the patient often has hours alone with nothing to look at but the walls, and a perfectly beautiful mix of flowers is glorious relief. A good rule-of-thumb for hospital flowers is to avoid fragrance and to choose bright, clear colors. For example, poppies are perfect.

Sizable gifts of flowers can be sent between people who know each other very well, on occasions that merit festivity or congratulations or unabashed overindulgence. Otherwise they are often simply misguided and out of place.

me branching foliage with the long flower stems whenever possible. Cut late on a Sunday afternoon, they arrived Monday morning. I put them immediately into buckets of very warm water and placed them near radiators, for they needed to be at their very peak but one short day later.

I mixed masses of perfect full-blown flowers with imperfect branches and yellowing leaves, various stages of ripening rose hips and fading flowers, and casually interwove them across three tall glass rectangles spread out along the showroom entry table.

Perhaps a picture *can* be worth a thousand words. In any event, it allowed Calvin to communicate to me exactly what he wanted, and it allowed me the chance to make a perfect result.

Learn to communicate. A single picture clipped from a French magazine led to the simple wedding setting we fashioned. "Gathered" looking bouquets of garden roses, Queen Anne's lace, and waxflower were attached to the pews just minutes before the guests arrived.

INSTEAD of developing rote responses and a set of prearranged selections to various situations, challenging our assumptions each time and working our way to each conclusion gives all of us the best chance to express our creative talents and to devise appropriate and personal offerings for our clients—even if we usually end up back at a similar place. From time to time, we might even surprise ourselves and come up with something innovative and completely original.

[Part Two]

SUPPLY ROUTES

A GALAXY OF CHOICES

[Chapter 2: What there is to find and

the many places you can find it]

MARKETS AND STORES

BEFORE THE MARKETS: Where do most commercial flowers come from? Which flowers are grown and why?

Perhaps we should demystify the business side of flower growing by observing that, like any other crop, cut flowers are farmed. Flower varieties are selected and grown for certain primary attributes, that is to say, in response to certain pressures from the growing process *and* from the marketplace. In addition to aesthetic criteria and consumer demand, fresh-flower varieties are selected and grown for the following reasons: ease in growing, packing, and shipping; predictability and uniformity of the end product; and longevity.

While these considerations are undeniably important, none of them necessarily produces a more beautiful flower. Achieving some of them, in fact, eliminates the very qualities that often make flowers so interesting.

Let's begin with the issue of transportation. When packing and shipping

It's a race against time. Flowers bought early in the morning are just hours away from their final destinations. **OPPOSITE:** *Near Lisse, the dazzling geometry of the Dutch flower fields stretches as far as the eye can see.*

considerations become a *defining reason* for how and why a flower is grown, much of the ultimate purpose of the flower has been subverted. The produce industry has yet to come up with the long-promised square tomato, developed specifically to pack more efficiently in a rectangular box, but the flower industry has often grown flowers with an eye to how they best fill a packing crate. Since straight stems of uniform height fit most snugly in a box, this is what many commercial growers strive to produce. And while the industry has been very clever in handling certain technical problems—shipping gloriosa lilies in inflated conical plastic bags, for instance—more often than not, instead of accommodating the irregularity of flower shapes by devising better packing techniques, growers have produced flowers to fit the box.

But the garden seldom reveals anything with a straight stem. Since it is the Mädderlake aim to choose and fashion flowers to reflect the natural world, we note that many commercially grown flowers fail to approximate what we see and admire growing all around us, causing us to have to look elsewhere for material. So, some things gained perhaps, but some decidedly lost.

Perfect predictability every time no matter what the season is another somewhat understandable yearning of flower growers and sellers alike. It makes doing business infinitely easier. Unfortunately, scant few varieties can be produced with such assurances; those that can, dominate production.

Roses are a perfect example of a flower whose exceptional sensual qualities and enormous range of physical attributes have been diluted by the "need" to produce a completely predictable and uniform product. Thumb through any books on classic garden roses, then peruse the rose selection in any flower shop anywhere, ours included, and draw your own conclusions. The commercial houses grow in a very narrow band of the spectrum, and those of us who desire a more diverse offering have to struggle to increase the range.

Of course, when a consistent demand is voiced to the industry, changes can and will occur. Now, at least in a few urban markets, "garden roses" are available—roses that smell incredible; roses that open flat-out, petals arched back to reveal a glorious, fuzzy center or subtle nuances of shading; and roses with huge, oversized flowers or a single row of petals. Certain small producers—most notably in the Var region near Nice in France and in the Sonoma

PAGES 44 AND 45: Packed to the gills with vivid layers of chrysanthemums and carnations, a truck at the Aalsmeer market is ready to roll. The delicate French field poppies are an option not offered at Aalsmeer. **PREVIOUS PAGES:** *A flower seller hawks his wares on the Spanish Steps in Rome. Selections from Tokyo's wholesale market are en route to a local shop.*

Valley in California—ship exquisite varieties: the French rose 'Marclla', for example, displaying soft shadings of yellow to butterscotch to burnt rouge; or from California, the peony-shaped branch rose called 'Abraham Darby', whose flowers, looking like layers and layers of crinolines, shade from a faded cream on the outside to a blush at the center.

It continues to amaze and discourage us that so little of what is extraordinary in the flower world makes it into commercial production, and that so much of what is produced has a uniformity that in no way reveals the richness of its origins.

Finally, our common insistence over the years that longevity be the primary attribute of a cut flower has probably been the main determinant of the bulk of what has been grown and produced for sale. Quite frankly, having seen the damage this requirement has exacted on the industry, I think we ought to begin to soft-pedal it a bit, convincing customers that the trade-off is seldom worth it. Consumers ask no more than a couple of hours from a great bottle of wine or a perfectly roasted red snapper. Why must all flowers have to last weeks?

PROFESSIONAL FLORISTS don't have to be left out of this largesse. It's easy to make contact with area farmers and ensure a supply of garden flowers by buying directly from a grower. Or, as they now do in New York, vendors in the wholesale markets can make arrangements to represent the wares of farmers and other cottage growers alongside their imported produce.

When longevity is the issue, certain flowers perform head and shoulders over others, so it's no wonder that wherever we go, we seem to see the same few flowers offered for sale. Only the most adventurous among us choose to experiment with the intrigue of the less known. But isn't it true that the delight of living in this world lies in exploring its diversity, not in narrowing its possibilities? With the realm of flowers made up of tens of thousands of varieties, how can we have ended up with so few with which to grace our everyday lives? Could our growing and selling criteria be somewhat out of touch with the times?

"If it ain't broke, don't fix it." Unfortunately, this nugget of homespun wisdom neatly sums up the current status of the flower industry's supply side, for until growers and suppliers of fresh flowers become aware that consumers are yearning for a more varied harvest, the flower crops will remain limited. On a somewhat brighter note, since flower sales are off worldwide, recent rumblings indicate that many industry figures are concerned about the future direction of the flower business, although unsure quite what the problem is. **READ ON.**

The markets of the world are driven by consumer demand. If there ever were to be raised a distinctly audible voice for a more dramatic range of fresh flowers, they would begin to appear, no matter what problems the industry faces in growing them and getting them there.

The Greatest Market on Earth

There is nothing remotely like it anywhere else in the world. Bathed in an unflattering greenish fluorescent pallor, it is not beautiful, but a massive, impressive, awesome sight.

Located on the outskirts of Amsterdam, the vast flower halls of Aalsmeer house the extremely efficient machine that catalogs, displays, sells, packs, and distributes flowers from such diverse places as New Zealand, Israel, the Netherlands, France, England, Germany, and Kenya to its own constituency as well as to the United States, Japan, and the rest of the world.

At no one point can the eye begin to take in the endless stretches of fresh,

OPPOSITE: *Not for the faint-of-heart, the giant Aalsmeer auction is the daily Dutch version of "Beat the Clock." In one day, more than 12 million cut flowers are hauled through these halls. Neatly crated merchandise seems to stretch endlessly in all directions. A litter of bikes crowds the entrance to one of the thirteen auction chambers.*

[Why Prices Fluctuate]

If a buyer has a firm order from a client for a huge quantity of one kind of flower, he almost has to buy it at a top price in order to ensure that he can fill the order. The double-digit cost of Valentine's Day roses comes straight out of this system. Everyone is looking for the best flowers and buying at the top price in order to be sure of filling orders.

Look at what you can find from just
one producer.

'Ace of Hearts', 'Alec's Red', 'All That Jazz',
'Amber Queen', 'American Pride', 'Amiga Mia',
'Angel Face', 'Anna Pavlova', 'Apricot Nectar',
'Bambey', 'Berolina', 'Betty Prior', 'Bewitched',
'Blue Girl', 'Blue Nile', 'Blue Ribbon', 'Brandy',
'Bride's Dream', 'Brigadoon', 'Broadway',
'Brown Velvet', 'Captain Harry Stebbings',
'Cathedral', 'Champagner', 'Chicago Peace',
'Chrysler Imperial', 'Class Act', 'Crimson Glory',
'Dainty Bess', 'Double Delight', 'Dublin', 'Duet',
'Dutch Gold', 'Eiffel Tower', 'English Miss',
'Evening Star', 'Everest Double Fragrance',
'Festival Fanfare', 'First Love', 'First Prize',
'Folklore', 'Fountain Square', 'Fragrant Cloud',
'French Lace', 'Garden Party', 'Gardens of the
World', 'Gene Boerner', 'Glory Days', 'Gold
Medal', 'Golden Masterpiece', 'Golden Wings',
'Graceland', 'Granada', 'Grandpa Dickson',
'Greensleeves', 'Harry Wheatcroft', 'Headliner',
'Heirloom', 'Honor', 'Iceberg', 'Impatient',
'Ingrid Bergman', 'Intrigue', 'Julia's Rose', 'Just
Joey', 'Kardinal', 'Keepsake', 'King's Ransom',
'Koppies', 'Lady Rose', 'Lady X', 'Lagerfield'
'Lanvin', 'Leigh Lo', 'Lemon Sherbert', 'Lilac
Charm', 'Lili Marlene', 'Limelight', 'Little
Darling', 'Lobo', 'Louisville Lady', 'Love', 'Maid
of Honor', 'Margaret Merril', 'Maytime',
'Medallion', 'Michelle Meilland', 'Mirandy',
'Miss All-American Beauty', 'Mr. Lincoln',
'Natali', 'Neon Lights', 'Oklahoma', 'Oldtimer',
'Ole', 'Olympiad', 'Orange Sensation', 'Papa
Meilland', 'Paradise', 'Pascali', 'Peace',
'Peaudouce', 'Peer Gynt', 'Perfect Moment',
'Polar Star', 'Precious Plantinum', 'Priscilla
Burton', 'Princess de Monaco', 'Pristine',
'Prominent', 'Red Devil', 'Red Masterpiece',
'Royal Ascot', 'Royal Highness', 'Rubaiyat',
'Saratoga', 'Sea Pearl', 'Seashell', 'Senator
Burda', 'Sexy Rexy', 'Sheer Bliss','Sheer
Elegance', 'Shining Hour', 'Showy Gold',
'Smoky', 'Smooth Prince', 'Sonia', 'Spanish
Sun', 'Spellcaster', 'Stephen's Big Purple',
'Sterling Silver', 'Suffolk', 'Summer Dream',

neatly carted merchandise. Pedestrian communication is strung out along two seemingly endless spines suspended high above the bustling floor below. As with any auction, timing is of the essence. Bicycles hastily strewn about at the doors to the numerous auction rooms testify to the speed with which buyers must get themselves into position for the next round of sales.

The system is deceptively simple. Flowers are logged in, categorized into selling lots, and placed in identical stainless-steel carts, all available for inspection by the buyers. Eventually they are hooked up to an automated track system that will draw them through one of the numerous auction rooms. Once each lot of flowers reaches the auction floor, the electronic seconds of a giant clock on the wall begin to decline, tumbling the value of the lot by the second. The longer the flowers remain unsold, the lower the price. The first buyer to touch the button located at his seat stops the clock and buys the lot. While the trick is to pay as little as possible without losing the sale to someone else, the better the quality of the flowers, or the more demand there is for a certain variety, the more pressure there is to react quickly. The sheer volume sold and the speed with which it's all dispatched is numbing.

Wholesale Markets

A florist's search for fresh flowers begins with the regional wholesale markets. Though a handful we've encountered in our travels do mount a dazzling daily haul and serve it up with spirit and a sense of camaraderie to boot, all too often the overall selection is disappointing.

By a wide margin, the greatest wholesale market we ever visited was the vast terminal at Rungis, just south of the city of Paris. Here the selection is always varied, sometimes even astounding, but more important one finds a pervasive and palpable warmth and joy in the act and the art of selling flowers. Whereas most big markets sell in bulk out of the boxes in which the produce arrives, here at Rungis each vendor displays his wares in his own fashion, with pride and personal flair. It was amazing and heartening for us to see that people who have sold vast quantities of flowers every day of their lives can still recognize the beauty and the seductive qualities of their wares.

'Summer Fashion', 'Sunny June' 'Sunsprite' ('Friesa'), 'Sweet Afton', 'Tabris', 'Tiffany', 'Tiger Tail', 'Tropicana', 'Viva', 'Voodoo', 'White Delight', 'White Knight', 'White Lightnin', 'White Wings', 'Yves Piaget'

[ENGLISH ROSES] 'Abraham Darby', 'Allux Symphony', 'Ambridge Rose', 'Belle Story', 'Bredonne', 'Brother Cadfael', 'Canterbury', 'Charles Rennie Macintosh', 'Charmian', 'Chaucer', 'Chianti', 'Claire Rose', 'Cympaline', 'Dapple Dawn', 'Ellen', 'Emanuel', 'English Elegance', 'Fair Bianca', 'Fisherman's Friend', 'Gertrude Jekyll', 'Graham Thomas', 'Heritage', 'Hero', 'Hilda Murrell', 'Immortal Juno', 'Jayne Austin', 'Kathryn Morley', 'Leander', 'Lillian Austin', 'Lordly Oberson', 'Lucetta', 'L. D. Braithwaite', 'Mary Rose', 'Mary Webb', 'Othello', 'Peach Blossom', 'Perdita', 'Potter & Moore', 'Red Coat', 'Sir Clough', 'Sir Walter Raleigh', 'St. Cecilia', 'Sweet Juliette', 'Tamora', 'The Miller', 'The Prince', 'The Reeve', 'The Squire', 'The Yeoman', 'Wenloch', 'White Mary Rose', 'Wife of Bath', 'William Shakespeare', 'Wise Portia'

[OLD GARDEN ROSES] 'American Beauty', 'Apothecary', 'Arrillaga', 'Autumn Damask', 'Belle de Crecy', 'Camieux', 'Cardinal de Richelieu', 'Celsiana', 'Centifolia', 'Charles de Mills', 'Constance Spry', 'De Meaux', 'Duchess de Montebello', 'Fantin Latour', 'Ferdinand Prichard', 'Henri Martin', 'Heroine de Vaucluse', 'Konig von Danemark', 'La Noblesse', 'La Reine', 'Marchioness of Lorne', 'Mdm. Ernest Calvat', 'Mdm. Isaac Piereire', 'Mdm. Lagrasse St. Germa', 'Mdm. Pierre Oger', 'Mdm. Plantier', 'Mrs. John Laing', 'Nuits de Young', 'Oscar Cordel', 'Paul Neyron', 'Paul's Early Blush', 'Prince Camille Rohan', 'Reine des Violettes', 'Rosa Mundi', 'Rose de Rescht', 'Souvenie de Malmaison', 'The Bishop', 'Tour de Malakoff', 'Tricolor de Flandre', 'Tuscany', 'Tuscany Superb', 'Waldfee', 'York & Lancaster'

OPPOSITE: *A Parisian vendor presides over his roses in the great whole-sale terminal.* LEFT: *Potted Icelandic poppies in sleeves of white paper, ready to hit the shops.*

In the past few years I've had the chance to crisscross the country and found it hard to distinguish one city's market from another. I was perplexed. With a country as diverse as ours, with growing climates and ecosystems running through a multitude of climatic zones, why aren't each region's eccentricities found better reflected in its flower markets, as they most certainly are in its produce markets?

Our New York market is a bittersweet affair, with isolated pockets of greatness and spirit sandwiched between mediocre vendors who are interested mostly in turning a fast buck. The best vendors provide an abundance of choice and variety. Here are a few highlights from the New York market.

WHEREAS many wholesalers stick with the same old tried-and-true roses, year in and year out, Dutch Flower Line offers a variety that changes *from week to week*. Take a long look at their spring rose list:

FROM SOUTH AMERICA
'Barok', 'Contesse', 'Dallas', 'Dolores', 'Fire Ice', 'Harmony', 'Josepha', 'Majolika', 'Mme Delbard', 'Osiana', 'Tanja Spray', 'Teatime'

FROM CONNECTICUT
'Abraham Darby', 'Bredonne', 'Daffodil', 'English Garden', 'Fair Bianca', 'Perdita'

FROM ITALY
'Serena'

FROM FRANCE
'Anna', 'Greta Garbo', 'Harmony', 'Josepha', 'Marella', 'Madame Pompadour', 'Tango'

FROM HOLLAND
'Ajax', 'Arianne', 'Astra', 'Baccara', 'Bahama', 'Barcarola', 'Barok', 'Bridal Pink', 'Calypso', 'Caroline', 'Champagne', 'Confetti', 'Darling', 'Deep Purple', 'Diadem', 'Dorus Rykes', 'Eveline', 'Gabrielle', 'Garnette', 'Gerdo', 'Jacaranda', 'Jack Frost', 'Kiss', 'L. Silver', 'Mandela', 'Melody', 'Minuette', 'Nicole', 'Noblesse', 'Osiana', 'Parco', 'Porcelina', 'Rosario', 'Settyna', 'Sterling Silver', 'Texas', 'Tineke', 'Vicky Brown', 'Vivaldi'

scabiosa

celosia: *pink, violet*

campanula: *soft pink*

monarda: *burgundy*

agertum: *'Blue Horizon'*

astilbe: *'Amethyst', 'Peach Blossom'*

tulip: *'American Beauty', 'Rosario', 'Silentia'*

freesia: *'Cote d'Azur', 'Elegance', 'Golden Crown'*

rudbeckia: *black*

microcarnations: *cream*

roses: *'Anna', 'Chique', 'Lola', 'Majolika', 'Mandela', 'Mimi', 'Mme Delbard', 'Osiana', 'Porcelina', 'Princess', 'Privé', 'Rendezvous', 'Ruhland', 'Serena', 'Shadow', 'Souvenir', 'Tango', 'Texas'*

FROM CALIFORNIA

trollius, silene, scabiosa, saponaria, stock, sunflower, pitcher plant, sandersonia, poppy pods, artemisia, salvia, myrtle, lavender, foxglove, dill, fennel, hybrid delphinium, cornflower, calendula, *Statice latifolia*, godetia, tweedia, mini calla lily, bush ivy, horsetail reed, didiscus, gardenia, stephanotis, cymbidium

roses: *'Bonnie', 'Bridal Pink', 'Butterscotch', 'Candia', 'Cardinal', 'Champagne', 'Chantilly Lace', 'Delores', 'Fire and Ice', 'Golden Wave', 'Kria', 'Levande', 'Minuette', 'Mme Violet', 'Peppermint Swirl', 'Polka', 'Privé', 'Sizzler', 'Sonia', 'Sterling Silver', 'Woburn Abbey'*

FROM ITS THREE storefronts, *Fischer & Page* offers a complete selection of floral merchandise, from seasonal plants of all kinds to a large variety of dried materials to a phenomenal selection of fresh-cut branches and flowers. Here's a partial list from just *one day*:

GROWN ON THEIR FARM

lilies: *'Avignon', 'Belvedere', 'Casa Rosa', 'Casablanca', 'Easter', 'Elite orange', 'Fresco', 'Geneva', 'Glostripe', 'Hit Parade', 'Impressive', 'Laura Lee', 'Menton', 'Monta Rosa', 'Montenegro', 'My Romance', 'Polyanna', 'Sancerre', 'Santé', 'Stargazer', 'Tender', 'Toscana'*

allium, alstroemeria, angelica, coreopsis, delphinium, loosetrife, rudbeckia, snapdragon, sweet pea, veronica, yarrow

IMPORTED FROM HOLLAND

sweet pea: *purple, lavender, red, cream, white, salmon, blue, pink*

iris: *casablanca, purple*

lysimachia

Six days a week, fifty-two weeks a year, Parisian wholesalers display their wares with flash and flair. Hybrid sweet peas, OPPOSITE, *are fanned into a circle for easy picking.* ABOVE: *A golden sheaf of wheat separates red peonies from multicolored sweet Williams.* RIGHT: *Roses are piled high awaiting shipment.*

[*June 9, 1992—Caribbean Cuts: A Typical Day's Flower List with Provenance.* This *is variety.*]

Austria—AU/Brazil—BR/California—CA/
Connecticut—CT/Costa Rica—CR/
Dominican Republic—DR/Florida—FL/
France—FR/Hawaii—HI/Holland—HO/
Israel—IS/Italy—IT/Ivory Coast—IC/
Louisiana—LA/Michigan—MI/New Jersey—
NJ/New York—NY/North Carolina—NC/
Oregon—OR/Puerto Rico—PR/Singapore—
SI/South America—SA/Spain—SP/
Thailand—TH/Trinidad—TR

FLOWERS

agapanthus CA; alstroemeria HO; amaranthus CA; anthuriums: small, medium, and large; red, pink, and white DR/TR; astilbe HO; banana clusters PR; bells-of-Ireland CA; bird-of-paradise SP; brodiaea HO; bromeliad HI/HO/PR; calathea PR; calla lilies: red, yellow, and cream CA; campanula CA/HO; cassia CA; chrysanthemums BR/HO; daisies, feverfew, chamomile CA; delphinium CA/FL; dill, fennel (six feet tall) CA; dusty-miller HO; *Euphorbia fulgens*; (scarlet-plume) CA/HO; freesia FL/HO; freeze-dried fruits and vegetables: strawberries, kiwis, orange slices, broccoli CA; fresh hydrangea CA/CT/NY; gardenias (boxed) CA; giant flowering onion CA/HO; giant purple artichokes CA; gingers: Costus, 'Jungle King', Spectabilis, 'Tahitian', Torch, Wax PR; gloriosa lily HO; godetia CA; heather AU; heliconias: 'Dancing Lady', 'Parrot', 'Lobster', 'Rhizzo', 'Yellow Caribbean' PR; iris CA; kangaroo-paw CA; lavender CA; liatris IS; lilac CT; lilies: Asiatic, 'Rubrum', white CA/CR/HO; lily-of-the-valley CT/HO; lisianthus CA/FL/HO; miniature pineapples CR/IC; mint CA; monkshood HO ; nerine lilies HO; orchid sprays: aranda, miniature and large cymbidiums, dendrobium, oncidium, paphiopedilum, phalaenopsis, vanda HI/HO/NJ/PR/SI/TH; ornithogalum CR; peonies CA/CT/HO/MI/OR; phlox HO; poppies: California, Oriental CA; protea: banksia, king, leucodendron, mink, pincushion AU/CA; Queen-Anne's-lace NY; rosemary CA; roses CA/CT/HO; safflower CA; salvia CA; saponaria CA; sarracenia LA; scabiosa CA; 'September weed' CA/HO; solidaster/solidago IS; statice CA/SA; stock CA; strawflower CA; sunflower CA/NJ; sweet pea (hybrid and wild varieties) CA/CT; sweet William NJ; thistle CA/HO; tulips FR/HO; tweedia CA; viburnum (seven varieties) NJ; waxflower AU; yarrow CA.

FOLIAGE

ape leaves (giant alocasia) FL; asparagus fern PR; bamboo poles, 3–4" thick, 8' tall (Buddha's-belly) HI/PR; bay branches CA; bear grass CA; berry branches: blueberry, pepperberry FL/NY; branches: honeysuckle, willow, wisteria NJ; kiwi CA; camellia branches (with and without flowers) CA; calathea PR; cattail CA/NJ/PR; cecropia (giant leaves) DR/PR; coconut flowers PR; coconut sprouts PR; croton leaves PR; cut ivies (seven varieties) CT/NY; dieffenbachia HI/PR; dock NJ; eucalyptus pods and branches CA/PR; evergreen branches: yew OR; fern fronds: maidenhair, tree fern, woodwardia FL/PR; flox (sword-shaped desert foliage) CA; ginger leaves PR; horsetail reed CA; jasmine branches CA; lemon leaves CA; monstera leaves CR/HI/PR; myrtle CA; orchid grass HI/PR; palmetto FL; pinecones CA/NC/PR; pittosporum branches CA; protea foliage AU/CA/HI; rain capes NJ; ruscus IT; sheet moss, mound moss, deer moss, Spanish moss NC; ti cuttings and leaves HI/PR; wild grasses: rye, umbrella, wheat CA/CT; wreaths: bay, eucalyptus, wildflower CA

In Paris, flower stores run the gamut from the Left Bank's charming and very laid-back Passé Simple to the Right's elegant La Chaume. Shouldn't our stores show the same vitality and personality?

Ben Fischer has spent all of his life in the flower business. He lives and breathes flowers, works seven days a week, thrives on challenges, and will do almost anything to come up with the right goods.

He's a bluejeans-and-baseball-cap kind of guy who spends his morning hours in one of four storefronts his business occupies, bundling a seemingly endless parade of flowering branches and passeling them out to customers. Then he heads off in one direction or the other: South Jersey to cut rhododendron, to the mountains for wild azalea and clambering sweet pea, or to the farm to review the scores of flowering shrubs he has recently put into cultivation for cut flowers.

Listen to him.

Q Can you make money in the flower business?

A (emphatically) Yes. Maybe not the kind of money you can make in some other businesses, but yes. There's plenty of room for making good money in the flower business if you keep up with—make that, keep ahead of—what's going on.

Q You have, by far, the greatest range of choices in the New York market. How do you manage it?

A Since we're both direct importers *and* growers of fresh flowers, we've been able to dramatically increase the kinds of material we sell. We've got contracts all over the place— people cut for us, people grow for us, we grow for us.

Q Is there a good future for the flower industry in this country?

A Maybe yes, maybe no. Depends on whether we recognize that ideas about flowers are changing. There used to be scores of flower growers—big ones, too—but most of them have disappeared. Sometimes the real estate their ranges sat on just got to be too valuable and they couldn't afford not to shut down. But other times, they just didn't pay attention to how things were changing, and became obsolete. Dinosaurs.

There's a famous rose grower in Connecticut—big operation—who gave up a year or so ago after more than sixty years in the business. But he was still growing the same roses he started with despite all of the new varieties France and Holland have been shipping.

Now I hear that someone is going to reopen some of the ranges and grow these new ones. The only way to survive is to adapt to new tastes and times.

Q What's the most exciting part of the business for you?

A Finding new varieties to sell. That's our biggest push.

I gave the young guy who buys for us at Aalsmeer a video camera and instructed him to walk the length of the halls each day, aim the camera at anything he didn't know, and shoot a little film on it. Sometimes it's thirty seconds, sometimes it's three minutes. All new stuff. Then he packs the cassette in with the flower shipment and I can look at it the next day. This way, I keep up with everything that's going on.

Q What do you think of the regional wholesale markets around the country? Have you visited any of them?

A Actually I've been to a lot of them. They're missing out on a lot of opportunities.

Q Do you think that this situation could be changed?

A Easily. All those regions have got a lot of untapped resources. Every one of them has a wealth of native flowering shrubs and trees to cut from. It's just a matter that they either don't know or don't value that kind of merchandise. In any event, they could be ordering a whole different list of flowers from Holland.

Fresh from the grower, a hamper of sumptuous sweet Williams sits on the dock at Rungis.

Many storefronts are engineered simply to feed the voracious appetite of the corner grocery stores, packaging cheap bouquets in Mylar, mixing 'American Beauty' roses with baby's-breath, button mums with blue statice. Other houses supply an endless assortment of cut greens, many sold by the pound. The best of these houses now sell bales of flowering quince, dogwood, cherry, apple, and magnolia, and construct unusual wreaths and roping during the holidays: powder-blue spruce, double balsam, heavily berried juniper, boxwood combined with incense cedar, privet berry, winterberry, pepper berries, and rose hips.

Mixed in between, in an ascending hierarchy of vision, are the operations who cull flowers from Hawaii, South America, New Zealand, France, Israel, California, Florida, and Holland, each with its own particular method of buying and its own range of offerings. A few of them are spirited and magnificent. One delightful store that specializes in tropical materials might have, in addition to the ever-present orchids, anthuriums, and gingers, brownish-burgundy banana flowers attached to rows of ripening green fruit, pomegranate branches in flower with emerging orange fruit, and temperate shrubbery such as acacias of various sorts, three or four kinds of eucalyptus, and bottlebrush.

Farmer's Markets

In areas where florists stock only what they find at the wholesale houses, farm stands and farmer's markets can help fill in the gaps. Because farmers were never educated in growing florist flowers, they usually arrive with a motley assortment of buckets filled with fresh-picked garden and field flowers for sale. Although the situation may be changing a bit in certain areas of the country, we've found that it has been here, much more often than in the wholesale markets, where we could find the cosmos, dahlias, zinnias, geum, local lilacs and mountain laurels, trumpet lilies, giant sunflowers, cockscomb, lythrum, goldenrod, and other meadow flowers so important to our work.

It seems that these outsiders have learned that we New Yorkers yearn to get our hands on a little raw nature, no matter how small, and bring it into our city surrounds to refresh our memory of the distant countryside.

ATTENTION: WHOLESALE MARKETS SHOULD BE STRICTLY OFF-LIMITS TO THE PUBLIC. PERIOD. Sadly, in many cities this is not the case. Selling flowers at retail is difficult enough without having to compete with potential customers at wholesale. Small shops that are trying to build a thoughtful service business rely on a loyal customer base in order to support their endeavor.

As florists, we should monitor our markets and keep wholesalers in line, insisting that they sell only to valid flower customers and not to the general public. They need our support and we need their support in order to build stronger businesses. *When either side undermines the other, everyone suffers.*

Flower shops that attempt to rise above the tried-and-true formulas need a strategic level of customer support in order to offer a wider range of services, flower choices, and inventive work. For customers who are interested in a continuing and changing supply of interesting flowers, nothing is more important than finding a florist you admire and supporting him so that he, in turn, can serve you well. Customers who want to buy directly from producers should look to nearby farmer's markets.

In the best of all worlds, each individual florist would offer his own unique point of view, special flower choices, ways of combining and arranging flowers, and distinctive presentation and wrapping techniques, thereby presenting an array of interesting options to the consumer. We have a large selection of restaurants to choose from, why not a similar range of flower houses?

[*Lee Bailey*]

One of the real pleasures of living where I do in Manhattan is its proximity to Union Square, which is host to an open-air greenmarket four days a week during the summer months and three during winter. When I first moved here, the flowers seemed pretty much a second thought, what you'd expect to find at your local supermarket. But that began to change. More and more of those selling produce caught on to their customers' hunger not only for fresh vegetables but for simple, natural flowers as well. The upshot has been that now we're treated to a glorious mix of inexpensive country flowers side by side with the produce, from early spring right up to frost—and in the colder months, hothouse potted bulbs and small plants. Modest prices would be enough to tempt most people, but I'm certain it's the naturalness and garden familiarity that really make these flowers so appealing. For instance, in the fall you're likely to find generous mixed bouquets of wildflowers—asters, goldenrods, and field daisies—and in early spring, witch hazel, pussy willow, forsythia, and daffodils. In summer, as different varieties come into season, there's a constantly changing array of old cutting-garden

I'M NOT AN ELITIST and I'm all for appropriate flower resources for all incomes, and, yes, some fruit and vegetable markets do sell attractive flowers at a good price. But along with large grocery chains and card shops, many of these produce purveyors mirror the worst of our traditions, offering cheap flowers that look cheap. On the other hand, farmer's markets often sell flowers as cheaply as do these vendors, but oh, what a difference!

reliables such as zinnias, dahlias, salvia, and marigolds. They're a feast for the eyes and a lift for the spirits even if you don't buy.

While wandering around in the market early one morning, looking to see if one of the growers had brought in cut Queen-Anne's-lace like I'd bought the week before, I recalled something Tom Pritchard had once said to me when we were discussing store-bought flowers. "Just because flowers happen to be inexpensive," he said, "doesn't mean they have to *look* cheap." That's a good thought for us all to remember. When buying flowers, select those with character and naturalness. They don't have to be exotic, personality is enough.

Finally, I suppose that's what attracts me to the flowers I buy in the market. They are not uniform in size, and many are common species that the average florist doesn't bother with. Some even have a few bug-chewed leaves, but they look like, and remind me of, a garden. That's their character and that should be enough for anyone. It certainly is for me.

Lee Bailey is the author of Country Flowers *and* Small Bouquets

Hands down, farmer's markets all over the world win the prize for naturally grown flowers. It's about time mainstream florists caught on and caught up. Until then, consumers should look for the outdoor markets nearest you.

BEYOND THE MARKETS

THE RICHEST ALTERNATIVE SOURCE for finding fresh flowers may, oddly enough, also be the most affordable.

Throughout the year, nurseries and garden centers of all descriptions can provide flower arrangers with a wide selection of flowering plants from which to clip valuable and unusual arranging material. Even for professionals used to buying at wholesale prices, these sources often prove to be more than competitive. For instance, a creamy, sensuous climbing rose plant such as 'New Dawn' (a variety we've never encountered as a cut flower), with long, shapely branches, good foliage, and numerous sprays of flowers, might cost as little as $10. Depending on how it was cut, each branch with its multiple flowers might end up costing just a dollar or two. Or a rugosa rose with fifteen to twenty stems sporting bright orange to apple-green rose hips and deep magenta flowers might yield up its bounty for less than a dollar a cutting.

Like many of you, Mädderlake is often charged with making extraordinary work for large events—to give a wedding a personal look, to garnish a store opening with flowers unusual enough to catch the jaded eye, to make a presentation bouquet that stands out from all the others offered on stage. To do so, we head right to our roster of nurseries and contemplate the possibilities. Don't overlook anything; this kind of trade is as good for their business as it is for yours.

Cultivate special relationships with the garden centers that let you go into back rooms and other "off-limits" areas and buy or borrow special merchandise.

Don't overlook rental opportunities as well. A trellised confederate jasmine seven feet tall and loaded with thousands of delicate, fragrant white flowers, far too expensive to buy but affordable to rent, became the centerpiece of a wedding reception and also contributed its subtle, trailing flowers to the bride's bouquet.

PREVIOUS PAGES: *Look at the cutting possibilities in those potted roses! Once cut, set plants out to produce more blooms or give them to a friend with a garden. The love and care with which the pansies were dug and wrapped speaks volumes for those responsible. Learn to let flowers move you.* RIGHT: *Local nurseries and garden centers offer an unparalleled source for unusual fresh flower cuttings. Here, ready for the arranger's knife, are fuchsia, monbretia, tuberous begonias, three or four geranium varieties, roses, and mandevilla.*

Canterbury bells, grown from seed.

BELOW: *Rieger begonias are perfect for centerpiece work; cut them or use little potted plants on the table.* OPPOSITE: *This perennial produces strange translucent balls along the length of its branches.*

Pass nothing by. Look for unusual combinations and interesting ways of combining them. The green tomatoes we added to this arrangement of peonies and shapely nursery-grown fox-gloves—criss-crossed in two tall glass rectangles to double the size of the final mix—catch even the most jaded eyes.

Coupled with economy, since the selection in nurseries is usually far more interesting and varied than that in the flower markets, cutting from material bound for the garden can be both a bargain and a delight, bringing a seasonal palette of unusual offerings to the arranger's table.

The final plus in this trio of good news is that, once cut from, plants can be set out in one garden or another, and called upon over and over for future flower work or to give up their pleasures in other ways.

From late spring through midsummer, vivid waves of color blanket the weathered outdoor nursery benches, each lined with seed flats of tall, feathery pink, white, and deep purple cosmos; brilliant jewel-toned zinnias; hot-pink cleome; and bright yellow coreopsis—all waiting to be whisked away to a waiting summer garden. At a net unit cost far below what you might find at wholesale (that is, if flowers such as these could be found at wholesale), these bright, colorful cuttings, and many more like them, are a virtual steal.

Tubs of perennials yield similar results, especially later in the season after they've had a chance to produce loads of flowers. Delphiniums, foxgloves, scabiosas, campanulas of various sorts, rudbeckias, hollyhocks, bleeding-hearts, and trumpet lilies are all available in abundance in good nurseries and garden centers. For the best cutting possibilities, look for leggy plants—they'll have the longest stems and widest range of stem shapes. Compact plants are useless.

Flowering vines are another good plant to raid for cuttings: trumpet vine (burnt-orange flowers followed later in the season by clusters of fat green seedpods), wisteria, clematis of all sorts (both single and double flowers and also the tiny miniature varieties), climbing hydrangea, and fragrant honeysuckle are all perfect candidates for the knife.

At other times of the year, these are the places to find a supply of houseplants from which to cut. Rieger begonias, cyclamens, azaleas, streptocarpus, kalanchoes, and clerodendrums all can serve an arrangement well. Geraniums, a favorite of ours, are one of the most valuable but overlooked sources of material for flower arrangers. Most nurseries and garden centers grow them in all colors, shapes, and sizes. Left spaced out on sunny windowsills to flower late into the winter, geraniums are easy to keep and to care for. Tall, center stalks are a perfect way to start a large arranging project. Because geranium foliage is often so beautifully marked, leaves and smaller cuttings work well as a green base in table centerpieces; mid-size cuttings are appropriate for adding a special texture or value to a traditional mix. If flowers or branches are cut when the flower is in full bud with just one or two open blooms, the cutting will last as long as anything in the arrangement.

Don't overlook scented geraniums. The flowers may be much subtler than their brighter cousins, but the foliage is often distinctive, and the many fragrances they sport—apple, cinnamon, rose, lemon, nutmeg, and peppermint, among others—are remarkable.

cattleya—the traditional corsage flower; can be found branched with multiple flowers; the smaller varieties are easier to work with; incredible translucent jewel tones.

cymbidium—the miniature varieties are more graceful than the giants; look for relaxed, shapely, not stiff, straight stems.

dendrobuim—long sprays of pure white, deep magenta, or mixed colors; hybrid varieties run the gamut of brilliant two-toned colors.

epidendrum—long, arching stems with small orange flowers; they last forever and are great for adding exotic grace notes to a large mix.

oncidium—a large family of clear yellow and rusty brown flowers; long-lasting.

paphiopedilum—the lady-slippers; many interesting hybrids; the smaller and more delicate ones are the most graceful and witty-looking.

phalaenopsis—moth orchids; ubiquitous in white and shades of purple; the smaller ones are often more interesting.

vanda—spectacular markings and a wide range of strange colors from grayish purple to odd yellows and browns; production vandas are stiff and flat, but others have wonderful twisted shapes.

Orchids

Shipped from Thailand and Hawaii, Florida and California and Taiwan, orchid sprays are a mainstay of the flower business. Although many production orchids are stiff and straight and very unappealing, sprays cut from plants *can be* shapely and gorgeous. If the wholesale markets and importers don't provide them, find local growers and negotiate a supply of interesting shapes and varieties. Many local growers who sell small plants or who supply orchids for corsage and wedding work have benches of stock plants from which they could cut larger sprays. Others who keep "prize" plants for themselves—and these are often the most incredible shapes and colors—might be happy to sell some of their prize flowers on occasion. Remember, the longer and more shapely the stem, the more useful the orchid will be for the arranger.

ABOVE LEFT: *Stems of hybrid dendrobium cut from a plant.* LEFT: *That old corsage favorite—the cattleya—can be elegant and very stylish in a simple vase.* OPPOSITE: *"Transform the room into something she won't expect!" was the charge that led us to add feedbags and sensuous dendrobium orchids to the 21 Club menagerie.*

Stay alert for new materials and new combinations. A fruited passion-flower vine in a garden center in Italy caught our eye; a stolen branch added a surprising finish to the mix, **ABOVE**.

ADVENTURING IN SCOTLAND

[WHAT TO DO WHEN THE CUPBOARD IS BARE]

NOTHING COULD HAVE PREPARED US for our first view of Greywalls. Even though we were on a tight schedule and due to cross the channel to Europe in two days' time, the privilege of photographing flowers in a house designed by Sir Edwin Lutyens with gardens by the famed designer Gertrude Jekyll was worth the long night's drive to the eastern coast of Scotland.

We arrived at Greywalls at the end of the first week of June, hoping to find the gardens in full tilt. But as we turned into the drive, a sad story unfolded: the gardens were completely bare, devoid (or so it seemed) of leaf or flower. We later learned that an extremely fierce winter in this particular coastal region had set

PREVIOUS PAGE: *Who would have thought that common old garden variety myrtle could look so lovely in a vase?* ABOVE: *Our first grim view of Greywalls.* RIGHT: *Maybe we've all been too hard on the lowly dandelion.* OPPOSITE: *Branches cut from a fuchsia and a begonia add interest to a mixed arrangement.*

the seasons back six weeks, delaying the garden's progress and pretty much shattering any hope we had of making pictures.

Yet after a little reflection and a consultation with my traveling companion and photographer, Lang Clay, I determined not to let this great setting go to waste. After all, we *were* there. And so we set about to see what could be done when the cupboard seemed bare—as good a test as any for my notion that there's always something to find if only you look hard enough.

The gardens stretched green and brown in all directions, but the hillsides glowed a brilliant yellow with a native shrub called gorse. This was where we began. Gorse, it turns out, is as thorny as juniper, a real menace to the hands, and therefore required careful handling. At first glance, it looked messy and unusable, but I found that the dead matter that clogged each branch could be pulled out and discarded, leaving only perky yellow flowers. Also, each branch could be given an individual shape by cutting away extraneous pieces. Opening up the branches would also help establish a sense of interior space within the arrangement, a little breathing room so to speak, so that the flowers would not simply look thick, messy, and clumpy as they did on the hillside.

Having cut and cleaned a fair amount of the stuff, I rummaged through the kitchen shelves and found a large, oval, copper fish poacher into which I lodged individual branches in an irregular silhouette, taking care not to fill it too full. The resulting assemblage sat in the library on a low coffee table in front of a blazing fire.

Comments that evening from Greywalls' guests, ranging from "sunny and sporty" and "cheerful" to "rich and elegant," rewarded our choice. One guest even wondered if it was mimosa. But the most remarkable words came from our host himself, who, after saying how cozy the flowers made the room feel, wondered what they were and if we had brought them up with us from London.

We continued our search.

A closer look around the gardens revealed a marmalade shade of flowering quince in full clip, cowering against the warmth of a protected wall. Nearby, a pale blue vine called vitex—completely

new to me—sported subtle clusters of flowers resembling double grape hyacinths. There was potentilla in scraggly flower at one end of the garden and a few strands of the popcornlike flowers of Japanese kerria in bloom near the gatehouse. A small glasshouse at one end of the garden held a few sad geraniums and begonias, pretty unfortunate to look at but good enough to cut from.

In the nearby town, a local garden center with one plastic-covered hoophouse let us cut from a bergenia growing under a bench in the dirt floor, a jasmine in flower, a euphorbia of one kind or another, a delicate trailing fuchsia in full bloom, a forced spirea bush, and a tiny-leaved angel-wing begonia.

Back at Greywalls, further foraging revealed myrtle flowering under a blanket of thick green leaves—large cold flowers, on stems long enough to cut, in the deepest shade of ink blue I have ever seen.

A nearby apple tree gave up a few short branches of blossoms not hit by the late cold. And the sunny yellow dandelions, fat and juicy and scattered about in great numbers, made a cheery addition to our luncheon table.

Just remember—there's always someplace to turn, even in the bleakest of conditions. When the cupboard seems bare, look someplace other than the cupboard.

Don't overlook what is right under your nose. I did. It took two days until it suddenly dawned on me that the yellow glow on the distant hillside might have some meaning at home. Just remember, when dealing with gorse—Scotland's native shrub—and other thorny branches, wear gloves and a long-sleeved shirt. Clip out dried matter and shape the branches before using.

Don't get discouraged in your pursuits; just look a little harder. Once found, cleaned, and carefully assembled, the hidden quince, BELOW, looked stately in the study, LEFT. Though a little inconsequential outdoors perhaps, the snippets of apple flowers and vitex, BOTTOM, will be welcome in more cozy settings inside the house.

Even the sodden little rhododendron hedge, LEFT, *gave up a few unspoiled blooms, just enough to garnish a writing desk,* ABOVE.

The few strands of kerria
flowers that actually
bloomed at the gate,
BELOW, helped enliven the
pitcher of white flowers
we left for the gatekeeper's
wife, LEFT.

[*Chapter 4: Raiding yard and garden*]

LOOKING OUTDOORS

WHAT IS CLOSEST AT HAND is often the hardest for us to see. We get so used to looking at the world around us in certain ways that, until we're jogged a bit, we sometimes don't see some of the perfectly obvious things.

I include myself in that indictment. I was very surprised to learn, several summers ago, that the catalpa tree that has towered over our country yard for the ten years we have lived there produces the most delicate and jewel-like flowers—undistinguished and unremarkable high overhead but exquisite up close. I had raked up those shriveled, fallen flowers for years without ever giving a thought as to how they might look freshly cut and placed on the table. One late spring day a storm brought down a branch, and I was startled to see how delicately drawn each of the flowers was, with subtle throat markings of deep yellow, a hint of blue, patterned with little black lines. Five or six clusters of flowers—their stem ends split and mashed—put into a low glass bowl looked remarkable and lasted five days.

[Some Branches to Cut From]

apple—these delicate flowers last only a short time; cut branches of fruit at all stages, from emerging green to fall's red.

birch and willow—useful to the arranger when the catkins are forming.

catalpa—clusters of delicately shaded, orchidlike flowers.

cherry—single and double blooms; the weeping variety is extraordinary in large arrangements that can be placed high enough to accommodate the long hanging branches.

chestnut—conical-shaped clusters of delicate flowers.

cornelian cherry—flowers similar to those of some varieties of witch hazel.

crabapple——there are many varieties of crabapples that flower in a wide range of colors; most are profusely berried in the fall, bearing clusters of yellow or red fruit.

dogwood—branches of the Kousa variety are flat and sometimes difficult to use because they are so one-sided—in the fall the pendant fruit is strange and exotic looking. The Florida varieties are white through pink and coral to red—beautifully branched and perfect for arranging; look for clusters of oblong red berries in the fall.

eucalyptus—there are several varieties with fruit and good foliage; seeded eucalyptus is a staple of the flower markets.

hawthorn—flowers are white to red and the trees are heavily berried in the fall; branches are usually interesting shapes—clean out interior foliage to show the shape.

magnolia—saucer magnolia (soulangiana) in the North and grandiflora and virginiana in the South all have big flowers; the latter two are fragrant. Star magnolia flowers without its leaves; its spent flowers hang somewhat comically, as if they had "melted" on the branches.

mountain ash—spring flowers and clusters of orange berries in the fall.

olive—various olive species produce nicely shaped branches with gray-green foliage and clusters of small green fruit.

pear—the Bradford pear has especially sweet white flowers in the spring and extraordinarily shaded waxy foliage in the fall, sometimes, but not often, with tiny pears.

pepperberry—pendant and upright varieties have delicate gray-green foliage and clusters of tiny pink berries.

redbud—an early bloomer with dense clusters of vibrant purple-pink flowers clustered near the main stem. Deep pink flowers show before the leaves emerge.

witch hazel—winter flowering with strangely shaped pale-green to golden flower clusters held tightly along the branch; blooms without any leaves.

PAGE 81: *Viburnum, quince, magnolia, and rhododendron branches share a vase.* LEFT AND FAR LEFT: *Never stop looking. Who would have guessed that lodged high above in this common "weed" tree lurked such delicate and orchid-like blossoms? Lasted five days cut, too.*

For those lucky enough to live in close proximity to a yard or a garden, the possibilities are endless; it's just that many of us rarely consider cutting from that which we see in abundance all around us. One argument maintains that yard material is too common or too familiar, that flowers should come from elsewhere, not from our own surroundings. We heartily disagree. But even those who hold to this line of thinking might stop a minute and consider this: Taking a piece of something out of its normal context and deciding to put it into an entirely different context or to reconfigure its balance of parts can sometimes so alter our perception of it that it becomes new again.

Strands of andromeda flowers stripped of their leaves, then gathered into a bunch and nestled in a small container look as rare as lily-of-the-valley. When massed together without all their greenery, vibrantly hued rhododendron flowers make intense flower jewels, nothing at all like their presence in the yard. A branch or two of mock orange or ornamental quince, carefully cleaned and shaped to an elegant silhouette, highlights a lovely flowering line, once hidden in a normally clumpy bush.

Then, too, what we're used to seeing outdoors is sometimes astonishing when found in the house. A craggy branch cut from a tree laden with ripening apples and brought into the house becomes a wholly different object. It looks surprising in its new setting, familiar but noticeable and delightful.

While the treatment of some candidates will be obvious, others will take a little thought. If the branches are shapely, use them as is. Don't hesitate to trim excess green leaves to better show hidden flowers, or to reshape what you cut, discarding any part that is not pleasing. If the flowers are perky but the plant itself is not, cut the flowers and use them in a smaller way. Remember that almost any plant that has flowers, fruit, seeds, or berries can contribute something to an arrangement. Keep an eye out for intriguing possibilities throughout the year.

Flowering trees are an obvious source for spring flowers. In the summer, watch for newly formed fruit; later in the fall, check for ripening fruit and berries. Emerging greenery can also be brought into the house: a shapely branch carefully cut from a Japanese maple just beginning to set out its

[*Careful Cutting*]

We rely heavily on being able to cut from yards and gardens for our work. When we raid, we always cut from abundance, and always so that the purloined piece does not in any way disfigure what's left. Honest. In fact, we often cut from the back side or underside of a plant or bush, looking for long, shapely branches, not just the outer flower clusters.

For professionals eager to increase their supply of arranging materials and unable to easily do so through commercial means, a network of yards and gardens is a useful solution. This kind of agreement could be beneficial to both parties. Home gardeners are often happy to make extra income by selling a little of what they have. After all, careful pruning of shrubs and trees benefits the plants by encouraging new growth. All things are possible on both sides of the garden fence to those smart enough to want them.

Monet had the right idea—just outside his kitchen window, **ABOVE**, stretches a garden filled with cutting flower choices. A once-in-a-lifetime opportunity allowed us to cut from the garden and work in the kitchen. We quietly "borrowed" a pitcher from Monet's famous yellow dining room and filled it with bearded iris, foxglove, scabiosa, and lunaria flowers and set it outside on the kitchen sill.

[Some Shrubs to Cut From]

abelia—delicate pink flowers on pendant branches.

acacia—several varieties produce good cut flowers, although the peak of bloom is brief.

andromeda—clusters of pendant flowers similar to lily-of-the-valley.

azalea—one of the most useful flowers for any arranger, from greenhouse-grown to yard and garden plants. The smaller-flowered native varieties are delicate and extraordinary. The Exbury hybrids add a wild new range of color choices—strange shades of yellow, rose, and orange.

barberry—great shades of translucent fall colors, then oval red berries.

bayberry—stiff branches with clusters of chalky-blue berries in the fall. Good for use through the winter.

beautybush—flowers profusely with coral-pink bell-shaped flowers.

blueberry—beautifully shaped branches with little bell-like spring flowers and fruit—pale green in midsummer and chalky-blue clusters in the fall. Dwarf wild blueberries can be found at higher elevations.

buddleia—a tall, rampant bloomer. Prune out spent flowers as the season goes on.

callicarpa—clusters of bright purple berries that grow close to the main stems; the native shrubs produce shapely branches, but production callicarpa is grown perfectly straight.

caragana (Siberian Pea)—soft pendant branches with yellow flowers.

chokecherry—a native shrub with white flowers and red berries.

cotoneaster—interesting shapes, especially useful for low centerpieces; small white flowers in the spring and various-sized berries in the fall.

crape myrtle—dense clusters of white to deep pink flowers.

cytisus (broom)—white, yellow to pink-purple flowers. Easily found in nurseries and useful for cutting.

daphne—delicately colored flower clusters; several varieties are extremely fragrant.

deutzia—gracilis has delicate white flowers; scabra sports more pendant clusters.

dwarf flowering almond—a profusion of pale pink flowers in the spring, though mostly on perfectly straight stems.

enkianthus—clusters of pendant, cream-colored, bell-shaped flowers.

euonymous—various forms, from climbers to shrubs; most useful for berry clusters in the fall; foliage on the wing-barked variety turns fire-red; texture of the branches is interesting after leaves fall. One variety sports hot-pink, three-sided seedpods that contain brilliant orange berries.

flowering quince—pale pink to deep coral flowers; cut in late summer for plump quince apples.

forsythia—the best branches for arranging come from shrubs starved for light, found deep in the shade or at the edge of the woods, and therefore with elongated, shapely branches and sparser flowers.

fothergilla—feathery white flowers in spring.

holly—many varieties and all produce berries. A staple of the Christmas season is winterberry, with bright red berries on naked stems; other hollies have different arrangements of berries and waxy green leaves. Our favorite is

American holly for its shapely branches, matte green leaves, and small red berries. The Japanese variety produces black fruit.

honeysuckle—shrubs produce creamy white to pink flowers in the spring and clusters of shiny red berries in the fall; vines produce delicate, fragrant flowers.

hydrangea—well known for their use as dried flowers, but they are also great as big and blowsy fresh flowers; shades of pink, blue, and creamy white; lace hydrangea is elegant and graceful.

Japanese kerria—a profusion of bright cadmium-yellow flowers that look like heavily buttered popcorn.

lilac—a staple of the cut-flower trade; in the spring five colors—white, lavender, wine, pale pink, and deep purple—are harvested in a wave up the East Coast, starting in the southern states and finishing in Maine. The season is thus extended to about nine to ten weeks.

mahonia—strange leaf clusters with pendant, vividly hued berry clusters in the fall.

mock orange—clusters of soft white flowers with tiny yellow centers.

mountain laurel—clusters of delicately marked flowers from white through pink to dark purple; exceptionally well-shaped branches.

nandina—clusters of white or red berries.

privet—tiny white flowers in early summer and dense clusters of blue-black berries in the fall.

pussy willow—although the common pussy willow has been worked to death, there are other varieties that are interesting, especially when the catkins are covered with yellow pollen.

pyracantha—spring flowers and bright orange fall berries; good branch shapes.

raspberry—wild and cultivated, these branches are most beautiful when loaded with ripening fruit. Colors from black to red and amber.

rhododendron—an incredible array of flower colors and a must for large arrangements.

Although the foliage has been a staple of markets for years, it's the flower clusters that are the prize.

skimmia—clusters of short, dark purple flowers that usually look much like double grape hyacinths but, on occasion, open and form four-petaled white flowers; now being produced for the commercial markets.

spirea—one of my favorites because bridal-wreath reminds me so vividly of growing up. There are several varieties, from pink to pure white, some of which are now being forced for the cut-flower market.

symphoricarpos—produces clusters of fat white berries that look like old-fashioned "gum-ball" chewing gum.

trumpet vine—the shapely flowers (a favorite of hummingbirds) have a subtle shading of pale orange to burnt red, and, like wisteria, the vine produces green bean pods from the flowers.

viburnum—there are many different forms and shapes of viburnum flowers, and certain varieties such as the "snowball" type are staples of the cut-flower market. All have interesting fall fruit.

weigela—branches laden with pink to red bell-shaped flowers.

wisteria—a flower that we're used to seeing scampering over trellises and hanging in trees but not in the house; it's interesting to isolate a flower or two in a small-necked bottle and bring it inside.

fringed trident leaves; the vivid, velvety apple-green buds of a nascent ornamental elm; a handful of willow branches with catkins just starting to drop,
unfurl, and fuzz up—all act as inside harbingers of what is going on in the
outdoor world.

Little needs to be said of the enormous possibilities to be found in cutting
gardens, herbaceous borders, or ornamental plantings, for surely those responsible for creating them are well aware of the prospects they offer for cutting
materials. But don't forget the vegetable garden if you want to add a surprising twist to your work. Tomatoes, eggplants, all sorts of squash and melons,
onions, nasturtiums, peas, and herbs each sport unique and delightful flowers,
ripening fruit, and shapely green leaves, lending whimsy and invention to the
arranger's bag of tricks.

Most gardeners have already seen the vision. It's the rest of us who need to
open our eyes just a little wider.

[Ken Druse]

My garden is small—around twenty feet by fifty feet. And yet I can nearly always find something to clip for a flower arrangement, or at least to add to purchased cut flowers. Even in winter, I can gather stems, twigs, and berries. Here's an example: one New Year's Eve I filled a bowl with light brown stems of deciduous holly covered with red berries, red-twig dogwood branches, the variegated gray-green and white ivy *Hedera helix* 'Glacier', dried oakleaf hydrangea blossoms, and sprigs of *Euonymus fortunei* 'Emerald Gaiety', whose leaves turn beet red in winter. *All* these plants came from the garden in winter.

Many trees and shrubs benefit from judicious winter pruning and yield interesting bark. Look to privet hedges in winter, for instance; the smooth beige bark is beautiful then. Young birch branches have bark much like that of a wild cherry: a shiny, rich red-brown. Their twiggy growth makes an attractive foil for cut flowers. If the winter hasn't been too severe, oakleaf hydrangea may have its burgundy fall foliage, but it will definitely have its wonderful shaggy, exfoliating bark, which looks like cinnamon sticks. Grape plants should be pruned before their leaves emerge, and their view are terrific in arrangements.

Then there are berries. A few clusters of magenta beautyberry may have eluded foraging critters or been spared damage from snow. Similarly, types of euonymus, viburnum, bitter-sweet, privet, barberry, bayberry, ivy, Virginia creeper, pyracantha, and hollies have persistent fruits. Some rose hips still hold in January.

Of course, leaves of evergreen and semiever-green shrubs and perennials can be called into service for natural arrangements. Consider the decorative unopened buds and broad leaves of mountain laurel. Leucothoe branches arch and are covered with lanceolate, pointed oval leaves that turn burgundy in winter. Bergenia leaves take on a coral cast in winter, often edged with magenta. Even pachysandra may be useful. Reach deep into the planting to find lower stems with leaves that haven't been burned by winter sun or wind.

Ken Druse is the author of The Natural Garden *and* The Natural Shade Garden.

[*Chapter 5: Cutting from nature and the wilds*]

INTO THE WOODS

OVERTAKING PATHWAYS AND ROADSIDES, scattered about the forest floor, and peppered through fields and country meadows are an abundance of woodland and wild flowers perfect for cutting.

Years ago Billy and I used to make weekend visits to our friend David's country house in the foothills of the Berkshires. Up the hill and beyond the ancient apple orchards in back of his house were vast stretches of wild blueberry, scrub oak, birch, and hemlock as far as the eye could see. On a long walk one day, we came to a large clearing that we'd never seen before, a flat, rocky terrain covered with wild potentilla, barberry, and red-twig dogwood and nestled next to a lazy pond surrounded by twisted mountain laurel, fallen trees, and frogs. In this clearing, and nowhere else about, we discovered legions of wild lady-slipper orchids standing upright in small outposts, quietly huddled under protective scrub. And scattered in between, brethren in this

ALTHOUGH the bounty of nature is available for our enjoyment, we must all take care to preserve whatever we find when we find it. It's important to learn to recognize endangered species and leave them growing. For instance, we would not hesitate to use the cultivated jack-in-the-pulpit or bloodroot plants we bought from a nursery, but we would *never* take them from nature.

PREVIOUS PAGE: *The extraordinary profile of one of our three surviving native American lilies.* FAR LEFT: *Stumbling upon a glade where flowers thrive naturally can be as moving as peering through the doors of a great cathedral.* LEFT AND ABOVE: *A swamp near our country house yields a dozen materials for a casual summer mix. Late fall bittersweet and crabapple branches,* BELOW, *strewn out on a kitchen floor. Watch it—if stepped on, they stain.*

*Look to summer's fields, too. These upbeat mustard flowers, **ABOVE**, were gathered near Dijon. **OPPOSITE**: Cut branches from various parts of a tree or bush for a variety of shapes; to avoid clogging, trim out the inner foliage and flowers before using.*

[*Transplanting Wildflowers*]

Do not attempt to move wildflowers from the woods to your garden, for most will perish from the shock. Although we feel that it is perfectly proper to cut wildflowers from abundant sources, the plants are essential to the food chain and must remain. Wildflowers provide nectar for birds, bees, and butterflies as well as fruit and seeds for birds and animals. Order garden wildflowers from seed catalogs.

solitude, were scores of tiny native lilies, each a bright orange trumpet-shaped flower whose shapely, slit-sided petals led to a yolk-yellow throat dotted with irregular black spots, moving gently in the slow cold breeze.

Like a remote treasure keep, these two unlikely rare flowers, a combination of strong shapes and values of purple and orange that would most certainly violate every rule in the flower arranger's manual, grew side by side in quiet splendor.

Although we were sorely tempted to "borrow" a few of these remarkable lilies, we left them to grow untouched. Several years later we stumbled across this same wild lily at a rare-plant nursery and bought five or six for our garden in New York state. Two or three have survived and to this day mark some of the best little moments of our summer garden. David died a few years ago, and in a certain way the tenacity of these remarkable flowers helps keep us reminded of him and connected to his memory.

Wild grapevines, bittersweet, cattails and marsh irises, vining honeysuckle, the little red and yellow woodland columbine, native grasses, wild phlox and sweet William, Queen-Anne's-lace, bishop's-weed, railroad Annie, wild sweet pea, and scores of other offerings are served up in various degrees throughout our surroundings. Rare flowers such as jack-in-the-pulpit, bloodroot, trillium, and wild orchids are best left alone.

Many wildflowers are tiny and subtle, and therefore not very useful for mixed flower arranging. But there are many places in the house that can offer a happy home to a small display: a bathroom sink, a windowsill, a writing desk, a shelf in the kitchen. Every flower lover should have a selection of little bottles, inkwells, or pottery vases to hold these small treasures.

But take from this domain carefully and with a regard for everyone else who shares in this common treasure.

In spring, the woods are full of flowering branches of all kinds, beginning with witch hazel, then redbud and a succession of wild fruit trees, ending in early summer with late varieties of dogwood. Wildflowers abound, from the tiny woodland delights of spring, through late summer and fall, when berries of all kinds begin to weigh the branches down with their ripening fruit.

[Forcing Branches]

One of the staples of winter's flower yield is the forced branch, and during January, February, and March, branches can be cut and brought straight into the house for forcing. Some good forcing candidates are witch hazel; fruit trees such as apple, crabapple, plum, and some cherries; dogwood; ornamental quince; magnolia; and forsythia. But you might try anything. Who knows.

Cut interesting, shapely branches that are heavily budded.

Place in room-temperature water in a warm environment. Change the water if it becomes cloudy. A little humidity helps keep emerging flowers plump.

Flower buds should begin to swell and open in about two weeks.

Remember that sunlight speeds development and deepens colors on some branches such as ornamental quince.

For early blooming (December and January—the dates depend on climatic conditions in your area), cut branches must be refrigerated to mimic the natural freezes of winter. This allows the branch to set or form its flower buds—a process probably best left to the professionals who are equipped to handle it.

There are so many varieties of wildflowers, it's hard to hold on to names for all of them. **ABOVE AND ABOVE RIGHT**: *Roadside pickings, simply arranged.* **RIGHT**: *A wintry assemblage of wild blackberries and heather, all found in southwestern France.* **OPPOSITE**: *Coral bells, sweet Williams, weigelia, and wild poppies share space with less familiar roadside picks.*

Learn to look near and far
for flower choices. The
garden gave up tall orange
frittelaria, but the distant
woods were filled with
naturalized daffodils and
currant bushes in flower.

ADVENTURING IN SAVANNAH

THE GREAT OUTDOORS TO THE RESCUE— ONCE AGAIN!

ABOVE: *Wisteria, plentiful all over the South, makes its way inside to grace a fancy urn in the hall,* OPPOSITE. *Since the urn is placed high on a pedestal, the draping form of the wisteria will work to good advantage.*

PREVIOUS PAGE: *Especially where flowers grow in great profusion, cut often for your flower work. Here, banksia roses tumble down a back alley wall in Savannah.*

ALL IN ALL, IT WAS BREATH-TAKING. Wisteria everywhere you looked, heavily laden with pale flowers, scrambling through trees and clinging to every limb and porch support. Creamy banksia roses smothered in tiny blooms tumbling like frothy waves over faded brick walls. Azaleas and rhododendrons of every shade and size blazing away. And all lit by a warm, sweet southern sun. But as lovely as Savannah was, it presented the same problems as did other cities around the States and in Europe: while the gardens, the woods, and the wilds were full to brimming, the normal sources for buying cut flowers had little that was interesting or inspiring. We had, however, timed our visit to coincide with azalea season and were fortunate to have plenty of flowers from which to choose. For even more variety, we scouted the various local nurseries and turned up a handful of interesting plants from which to cut.

Lang Clay and I arrived in town with a bag of camera equipment and a copy of *Flowers Rediscovered*, hoping that the city's reputation for hospitality would keep doors from slamming in our faces. Our plan was simple: We would first walk through the city's squares looking for the most attractive settings, then knock on a few choice doors and ask if we might take a picture or two inside. Sa-vannah natives are a flower-loving crowd, and all whom we met during our caper were intrigued with our mission and delighted to welcome us into their homes.

We first noticed a stately red-brick house, and when we determined that it was owned by a well-known antiquarian, we tracked him down at his store. No stranger to magazines and publicity of all sorts, he obliged our request without a second thought, and soon we were having trouble keeping up with the many treasures he kept offering to us to work with: the individual traveling tea service made for one of the czars of Russia, a table full of turn-of-the-century Baccarat glassware edged in pure gold, a seemingly endless array of beautifully furnished rooms of simple but stately elegance, and pantry shelves laden with china and interesting flower containers. The glorious bounty we had harvested from yards and gardens surrounding this little mansion, coupled with the warm light of a Savannah spring that flooded each beautiful room in its rosy glow, made our job sinfully easy.

As it turned out, we also had the privilege, through a friend of a friend, of working in the home of one of Savannah's noted flower arrangers. After we had photographed the dining room table centerpiece, I tackled a big silver trophy cup on a tall plant stand in a corner of the living room, determined to use a beautiful (and very expensive) bougainvillea I had bought. Starting with a branch of dogwood (cut from the lower reaches of a tree so that its form tumbled over the rim of the cup), I fashioned the rest of the mix out of long branches of weigela, a tiny-flowered native azalea, some garden and some market roses, and Queen-Anne's-lace.

As I was struggling with the last few flowers, my host entered the room, walked over, and regarded my efforts for a few moments. Finally, she exclaimed that it was perfectly beautiful. Exuberant, she added. That said, she proceeded to decry the fact that Savannah flower fanciers had so little variety from which to choose, just the "standard flowers" that one can get all over. "You people from New York are so lucky to have such an astonishing supply of varieties to choose from." Needless to say, she was surprised to learn that everything in my arrangements had been found within a mile of her house.

I made table flowers in both houses. Each had a formal dining room, elegant tableware, and footed silver containers—variations on a theme. I decided that both mixes should be made of fairly small-scale elements and be complicated in nature. One I meant to be a bit feisty and playful; the other was to

be reserved, with a little more decorum. For the latter arrangement, I limited my palette to a narrow range of muted colors and held the flowers fairly tight to the container, playing a game with small-scale flowers, many of which seemed but a variation of their neighbors.

To cover the foam brick, I placed branches cut from a white geranium and a small-leaved angel-wing begonia. Next, I added miniature pink azalea and clusters of delicate white flowers from a *Deutzia gracilis* shrub clipped from a nearby yard. The final additions were a tiny rose known as 'Pink Fairy' and a small pink thistle found in the wholesale market.

As I looked at the arrangement, I felt that it looked a bit bland, a little too controlled—I needed something to "throw it off" a little. The pale orange poppies that were left would have been perfect but were too large. Then it occurred to me that I could peel off the petals and use the fuzzy little yellow centers as a final grace note to the composition. They added just the right amount of fizz.

The second room was bolder and more daring and called for a splashier look, so I decided that the flowers for this beautiful vessel could be a little brassier in their shapes, mix of scales, and color. I began by cutting up some potted garden roses, using a cluster of

dark pink flowers to set the innermost value and trailing the remaining two or three branches down onto the table. To this I added pink geranium flowers and the little 'Pink Fairy' rose, and using branches cut from a climbing white rose ('Cherokee') found growing all over town, I began to sketch out the jagged silhouette of the arrangement, leaving plenty of room in the shadows for the only flowers I had carried down from the New York market, diminutive but perky Turk's-cap lilies.

Two rooms, two bowls, two settings, a decidedly different idea of what the flowers were to look like, and an understanding of how to go about doing it.

The flashy single rose
'Cherokee' that clambers
all over Savannah's gar-
dens and back alleys,
RIGHT, adds a grace note
to an antique store, FAR
RIGHT, and livens up the
woodsy tangle of pot-
grown roses, turks' cap
lilies, and geraniums I
made to tame the ex-
tremely elegant table
setting, LEFT AND ABOVE.

Be especially careful of side views. Remember that table flowers stare you right in the face, all through dinner. Here, I took care not to obscure the delicate beauty of this footed silver container. The spray rose 'pink fairy'— practically unnoticeable in the garden—ends up front and squarely center.

A dazzling assortment of spirited colors and elegant shapes, wisteria, geraniums, ranunculus, allium, anemones, and wild azaleas blend perfectly together in a footed porcelain urn.

[*Chapter 6: Cutting from the conservatory*]

UNDER GLASS

A FEW YEARS BACK, we had as a client a young Saudi Arabian prince of one rank or another. Needless to say, extravagance was often the order of the day, oil revenues being what they were—a situation that pleased us no end. Dinner parties at the prince's house were regal affairs; sixteen notable guests gathered around a huge dining table, the center of which was filled with more ornate silver objects than you could count or comprehend in an evening of sitting there. While the table flowers were often opulent and over-blown, and a treat to do, the more extravagant flowers were made in a pair of huge urns set in niches in the wall opposite the fireplace.

More often than not, we filled these stately urns with gnarled branches of magnolia or flowering quince, apple, pear, or almond, or, in the fall, fruit-laden apple or crabapple. The branches provided a structure or support for the other flowers. To them we would add the most colorful and exotic things we

Make combinations people will notice, BELOW. A silly stew of thumb-sized calamondin oranges, white bottlebrush, phlox, and deep yellow sandersonia made for a Bat Mitzvah caught and delighted everyone's eye. OPPOSITE: Tulips forced for London's great Chelsea Flower Show—now consigned to the take-home box— peaked a few days too early. OPPOSITE TOP: A young girl gets an escorted preview of the Show.

could find at the time: long, arching, flaming parrot tulips, for example, or wild, painterly Rembrandt tulips, or shapely scarlet azalea branches, or vivid climbing roses cut long enough to drape to the floor.

One day toward the end of February, the prince approached us with a bizarre request: "Would it be possible for you to make arrangements of ladies' earrings for my dinner party next week?" Of course we answered "yes," then asked ourselves what on earth we were to do, for this time we had drawn a complete blank. Finally, after some panic and some outlandish ideas about how to go about filling this request, we discovered that "ladies' earrings" is a common term for the hanging fuchsia plant, and this, of course, must be what our prince desired.

Though it was February, and most fuchsia plants were but a twinkle in their grower's eye, I remembered that the Philadelphia Flower Show was coming up, and that the previous year one of the growers had forced spectacular fuchsia baskets. Some detective work and help from the show's administrative headquarters led us to the grower, who once again had produced hanging plants with six-foot-long trailing branches laden with flowers, and, after a little coaxing, he promised us two, albeit at some hefty price.

Our "earrings" secured, we unpotted them, washed the dirt off the roots, then submerged one plant in each urn, threading the individual strands of two-toned flowers up into a network of supporting branches, looping each strand over a branch, and dangling the showy flowers like a multitude of brightly colored parachutes caught in the trees. So, for a king's ransom, we satisfied a prince.

We always have an eye peeled for exotic or unusual materials with which to fashion our work. Among the most intriguing resources we all have are the special flower and garden events that take place around the country, for quantities of unusual material are produced for the displays and much of this largesse is available before, during, and after the shows. In fact, with a little planning, you can coordinate with the participating growers, nurseries, and garden centers and get them to force your own needs alongside theirs.

Like most of the country's flower shows, the Philadelphia show, held when spring is still on everyone's wish list, is chock full of forced plant material:

rows of spectacular azaleas and rhododendrons in full tilt; towering magnolias and pears; clumps of aspens and silver birches; and acres of mature perennials—four-foot-high delphiniums, giant foxgloves, beds of astilbes, standard roses and climbing roses and miniature roses and tea roses and rambling roses. These exhibitors are often more than happy to rent or sell some of this production after the event and recoup a little of what they spent.

I made flowers for a bat mitzvah recently, something I had never done before. The girl being celebrated was strikingly beautiful, shy and forceful at the same time. The child in her still wanted balloons, but I wanted to play to the other voice, so I turned to a nearby winter hothouse for inspiration and found a host of unusual plants from which to cut.

I decided that the table arrangements should each be different, perhaps even a little irreverent, dotted with peculiar cuttings and flowers uncommon enough that kids and adults alike might really notice them. We began with

MANY GREENHOUSES and garden centers feature displays of "specimen-sized" tropical plants that benefit from regular pruning and shaping. If you spy something that might be intriguing to use in future work, ask if cuttings are ever available.

TANGERINE

Dallas Home & Garden Show,
Dallas, Texas; (214) 680-9995.

Indiana Flower & Patio Show,
Indianapolis, Indiana; (317) 255-4151.

Kansas City Flower, Lawn & Garden Show,
Kansas City, Missouri; (816) 444-3113.

Maryland Home & Flower Show,
Timonium, Maryland; (301) 969-8585.

Metropolitan Louisville Home,
Garden & Flower Show,
Louisville, Kentucky; (502) 429-6000.

New England Flower Show,
Boston, Massachusetts; (617) 536-9280.

New York Flower Show,
New York, New York; (212) 757-0915.

Philadelphia Flower Show,
Philadelphia, Pennsylvania; (215) 625-8250.

Pittsburgh Home & Garden Show,
Pittsburgh, Pennsylvania; (412) 922-4900.

Southern Home & Garden Show,
Mobile, Alabama; (205) 968-4600.

U.S. Botanical Garden Spring Flower Show,
Washington, D.C.; (202) 226-4082.

Washington Flower & Garden Show,
Washington, D.C.; (703) 569-7141.

APRIL

Ann Arbor Flower & Garden Show,
Saline, Michigan; (313) 998-7343.

San Francisco Landscape Garden Show,
San Francisco, California; (415) 750-5108.

St. Louis Flower Show,
St. Louis, Missouri; (314) 997-3407.

AUGUST

Southern California Home & Garden Show,
Anaheim, California; (714) 978-8888.

Massive shows of force: perfectly grown lupines at the Chelsea Flower Show. OPPOSITE: *Birds of a feather? No stranger to color himself, a Royal Pensioner seems quite naturally drawn to the tuberous begonia patch.*

[*Conservatory Cutting List*]

acacia	geranium
agapanthus	hibiscus
allamanda	jasmine
bamboo	loquat
begonia	mandevilla
bottlebrush	natál plum
bougainvillea	oleander
camellia	papyrus
clerodendron	passionflower
citrus plants	pittosporum
crepe mayrtle	pomegranate
cyperus	plumbago
eucalyptus	rapholepis
gardenia	sweet olive

ABOVE: *A lime plant, washed free of its dirt, is lodged, roots and all, into an old battery jar.*

OPPOSITE: *A dazzling array of greenhouse cuttings: plumbago, painted lady geraniums, lemon branches, and orchids join forces with market flowers like ranunculus, parrot tulips, poppies, anemones, phlox, and a brilliant, rather outspoken vermillion amaryllis.*

foliage cut from calamondin orange plants sporting white flowers and little fruits ranging from pale green to bright orange, heavily berried ivy we bought in the market, and cuttings from pink and white carnival-striped azaleas. To this we added greenhouse cuttings from a creamy white bottlebrush tree, finishing each arrangement off with miniature pineapples about the size of kumquats (grown on straight stems and looking much like swizzle sticks), branches of bell-like custard-yellow sandersonia, tufts of mimosa, garden phlox, hyacinths, and perky little orange-cupped narcissus—all assembled with a light hand.

It worked. The flowers brought just the right degree of playfulness and surprise to the tables—artful, kind of elegant, and amusing, all at the same time. Flowers perfectly fit for a growing-up kid.

We always move through winter conservatories and greenhouses with a sharp eye trained to what might look good in an arrangement. Branches of lemons and limes have almost become a trademark of our large work. But green plants with shapely leaves and a good branch structure are a perfect place to begin a large endeavor. *Ficus diversifolia* (mistletoe fig), especially when it's dotted along the length of the branch with pale brown nutlike fruit, and its cousin the edible fig—with large, bright green, quatrefoil leaves and sticky green fruit—both help make a backbone for the other flowers of a big mix. For trailing foliage, we cut from cissus or asparagus baskets. *Cissus discolor* sports incredibly marked, purple and white variegated leaves; *C. rotondifolia* produces a succulent leaf; *C. antarctica*'s leaves are oblong and saw-toothed; *Rhoicissus capensis*—a cousin of sorts—makes a leaf similar in appearance to a true grape. Asparagus fern (*Asparagus setaceus*) is a staple of many florists, but other varieties are intriguing as well. Meyer's asparagus—known as foxtail fern—produces thick, green, wavy spikes of plumage up to three feet long, while *A. sprengeri* makes bright green cascading branches sometimes dotted with pale green or bright red berries.

We find that even if a plant doesn't look like much in its own right, the pieces we cut, when added to a different setting, almost always contribute a substantial and appreciable presence.

WORKING

Part Three

UNDERSTAND WHY—THEN LEARN HOW

WITH FLOWERS

[*Chapter 7: Sorting through the flower selections and spotting new containers to hold them*]

MAKING CHOICES

Choosing Flowers

FLOWERS MUST BE SEEN to be bought. Having bought flowers in markets all over the world, we've found that it's not enough to develop a master list that eliminates uncared-for varieties and call it a day, for seasonal variations and different growing techniques produce flowers of vastly disparate looks and qualities all sold under the same name. Unless you're positively sure of your source, you can never buy just by the name of a particular flower.

Freesia is a good example. It's worth having when the individual flowers are plump and full and in good color, the stems shapely, and the succession of buds nicely arranged along the turned-down tip of the flower stem. At other times, its flowers flat or wrinkled and the colors washed out, it isn't worth a dime. The beauty of freesia lies in its sense of line, the grace of its form, its lyricism. What's the point if it simply looks knobby?

115

PAGES 112 AND 113: *Take a selection of flowering houseplants, use the same container for all three arrangements, but come up with a decidedly different mix for each.* PREVIOUS PAGES: *Your flower choices should move you to buy them. A hanging basket of campanula found in a green house near Loonen, Holland, was too beautiful to leave hanging; it fit perfectly in a coffee mug. A zany collection of garden cuttings meets its match in a pottery rooster.*

ALTHOUGH WE KNOW that many florists offer arrangements of flowers that seem to emanate from mounds of greenery contained in invisible holders, we feel that flowers are most appropriately presented either wrapped in clear cellophane or plain tissue to look like a gathered bouquet, or held in a simple container. Table centerpieces (as discussed later) are a notable exception.

Nothing is uglier than a badly grown tulip: spindly, with anemic, wilted, yellowing foliage and a thin, sad flower. Single and double tuberoses run the gamut from sensuous, gently curvaceous stems and full, creamy white flowers all the way to stiff, hard knots of bruised-looking brown flowers on thick, graceless stems. Ranunculus, tall and twisted of stem, with perfect foliage one week might come in short, stubby, and almost leafless the next. Delphinium can be elegant and graceful at times, compact and graceless at others.

Roses, lilies of all sorts, poppies, and many other varieties are often badly produced and thoroughly unattractive. Sometimes it's the fault of the grower or his techniques; at other times it may simply signal the very beginning or end of the growing season for that particular flower. In any event, always inspect the goods at hand before deciding if they're suitable for purchase or for your particular intentions.

Having discussed at length all the places where you might find flower choices, I should state unequivocally that it makes sense to work only with flowers that give *you* pleasure. Flowers chosen out of some sense of obligation or vogue will never add anything to your work. First and foremost, choose flowers that turn you on. You ought to be able to say to yourself, "These flowers are *really* beautiful." If you can't, consider looking elsewhere.

Before you buy, consider how the flowers are to be used. Flowers with a strong individual presence—large-headed lilies, gladiolas, hybrid delphiniums, liatris—are unlike most other flowers in their shape, their size, and sometimes their coloration and are therefore harder to combine than others. If a mixed arrangement is the goal, unless you've located flowers of similar hue and value, it might be better to skirt these choices in favor of flowers that share similar traits.

On the other hand, if a dramatic array of flowers of all one kind fits the bill, the giant stalks of deep purple, pale lavender, and royal blue delphiniums might be the choice, hands down.

We prefer flowers that develop with a sense of individuality—garden roses or poppies, for instance—rather than a sameness or uniformity—gerbera daisies and carnations. Each poppy is an individual, with its own unique shape,

CHOOSING and buying flowers at the wholesale level is an entirely different proposition from buying at retail. Professionals must learn to evaluate the quality of flowers that have just undergone a long period of transit and have been out of water for a number of hours and subjected to God knows what other conditions.

Flowers bought from boxes need to be carefully chosen, then appropriately marketed (that is to say, cleaned of excess leaves, re-cut, stems scraped) and put into buckets of water in order to allow them to regain their natural balance. Some flowers harvested in "tight bud"—so that they will pack without bruising the flowers—never develop as beautifully as flowers picked at a later moment in the flower's cycle. Single tuberoses picked after the flowers have started to open and carefully transported to the New York farmer's market in buckets of water develop far more beautifully and last longer than those shipped from abroad.

ABOVE: *Delicate, decidedly individual stems of 'co-quelicot', the famous French field poppies, sit in* *an etched glass pitcher.*
LEFT: *Soft and tender, an appealing little narcissus we found at a market in* *the English countryside ended up cut very short in a pleasingly battered silver cup.*

[*Pinching roses*]

Roses that feel mushy will probably wilt. The head of a rose should feel firm when squeezed gently between thumb and forefinger.

flower size, and stage of development, while each gerbera daisy looks identical to its neighbor.

Since the particular shape of each flower is of such concern to us, we've learned that we can buy certain varieties when they're produced in season from local growers, but almost never when they come from large commercial producers. Gladiolas are a perfect example. We find the stiff, upright, perfectly grown production gladiolas unwieldy and almost impossible to work with; however, we will snap up gorgeous, deeply colored, misshapen farmer's-market glads and delight in their almost comical, twisted individuality.

Choosing fresh flowers is pretty much like choosing fresh vegetables. Look for firm stems and firm flower heads. Just as with vegetables, avoid bruised or creased flowers. Fresh flowers *look* fresh. If it doesn't appeal to you, leave it behind.

There will be times when you may need the longest-stemmed flowers available, but, if possible, never buy longer than you actually require. Remember that you usually pay a premium for height. Remember, too, that tall flowers, fighting the force of gravity, have to expend more energy than shorter ones to keep themselves refreshed, thus shortening their life.

Look for flowers at the appropriate stage for your needs. If you're buying for immediate use, as we often are, you'll probably choose flowers that have already opened rather than tight flowers that will peak in three to four days. Nothing is more irritating than having party flowers open to their peak of bloom several days *after* the event. Buying flowers ahead of time and monitoring (encouraging or slowing) their development helps avoid this problem.

Learning to recognize fresh flowers isn't difficult, but it requires a little practice to be perfect. For the most part, though, it's pretty much a matter of common sense and a good eye.

[*Water Tubes*]

Small green-plastic vials with tight rubber stoppers allow florists to arrange flowers in places where containers don't fit. The citrus branches we used at the Palladium were the last element to be placed, removed from their buckets and water-tubed the afternoon of the party. Each tube provided just enough water to carry its branch through the next six hours.

Water tubes in several lengths and widths are available through many florists, garden centers, and crafts stores. Check the diameter of your stems and buy the appropriate sizes for your needs. A stem that takes up much of the room in the tube leaves little room for water. You can cheat by making a long diagonal cut along that part of the stem within the tube and eliminate up to half its bulk.

PROFESSIONALS: We emphasize again and again, at least to those who desire to rise above the herd, that since there are so many varieties of flowers available for using in arrangements, it is your particular set of choices and subsequent ways of combining them that give you the best chance to set your work apart from others.

Arranging flowers is a means of individual expression, and, as we state elsewhere, though we understand the reasoning behind the practice, we have never understood the value of standardizing flower arrangements and trafficking in the exact same choices as everyone else. Break out of the mold.

Whenever possible, buy closed flowers and watch them blossom. A sunflower spreads its petals then gradually fades until all that remains is the glorious seed pod. Daffodils, BELOW, won't age as beautifully.

Choosing Containers

Many flower books include chapters about finding containers, but the long and short of it is you can arrange beautiful flowers in just about anything. I made this claim during an interview for the *Los Angeles Herald Examiner.* "Prove it," they said and produced a thoroughly unattractive commercial coffee pot. Starting with a small branch of rose-of-Sharon I'd clipped from a bush outside the office and working with other "yard flowers" I'd found on the grounds nearby, I demonstrated, to their complete satisfaction, that it is the mix of ingredients, not the perfect choice of a holder, that matters the most.

There is a natural relationship to be found between a vessel that holds water and the flowers it contains. Both the physical characteristics of the container and the stylistic preconceptions you bring to your arrangement govern this relationship.

Very elegant florists often use visually "important" containers to hold their flowers. The windows of Maxim's flower shop in Paris or New York might present offerings of cymbidium orchids, corkscrew willow branches, and giant monstera leaves mounted in slender, curvaceous "art deco" vases three to four feet tall, or giant glass globes carefully arranged with a multitude of elegant calla lilies. La Chaume, probably the most elegant of Parisian shops, crams dozens of stems of garden lilies six and seven feet tall in that same slender vase, while on the floor below sits a huge, low-sided bowl glazed celadon green, packed with fifteen or more double-stalked apple blossom amaryllis, each surrounded by perfect emerald-green mound moss. The container is as much a feature of these compositions as the flowers: in other words, the flowers deliver part of their message by virtue of the container holding them.

Picture a tall, graceful bronze urn by Josef Hoffmann, beautifully ribbed and patinated, filled with a careful array of calla lilies or languorous French tulips. No matter what kinds of flowers are added to this vase, or how they are arranged, the presentation will be dominated by the visual presence of the elegant container. The same holds true for many silver or pottery vases: elaborate Victorian trophy cups, bowls, and flutes; strong, solid shapes from the Arts

[*Non-watertight Containers*]
To press a non-watertight container into service, simply find a liner of some sort that will slip inside. The liner could be anything from a paper or plastic cup to a drinking glass, kitchen bowl, or mason jar.

Floral-supply houses have various sizes of pressed cardboard liners, from thin conical shapes to large ribbed buckets. While many florists resort to these when there is absolutely no money in the budget for even a cheap container, they look hideous and should never be used if they will be seen.

Less sturdy but far less bulky, clear vinyl liners come in a range of sizes and can easily be trimmed with scissors to fit a variety of problem containers. For valuable pots and vases, consider finding a permanent liner, which will avoid the need for cleaning the vase itself.

Lighten up and have some fun with your choices. OPPOSITE: *This flea market soldier's head (an old Chia pot, we think) sports a cattleya hat and a silly grin; a spectacular tin sand pail,* ABOVE, *holds, sweet Williams with childish charm.*

Like these anemones, **BELOW,** *most natural flowers look perfectly comfortable in rustic holders; and the more choices, the merrier.* **OPPOSITE:** *A playful squirrel munches on nasturtiums; an antique redware strainer (lined) is filled with coreopsis; a Provençal jug contains flowering oregano; another redware piece is paired with grape hyacinths; and a bizarre carp vase devours a twisted gladiolus and a handful of agapanthus.*

and Crafts movement; curvilinear art deco vases—the container contributes a substantial visual value to the whole.

On the other hand, for those of us who work with flowers in what we are calling a "natural style," the flowers themselves are most decidedly given center stage. The container, rarely remarkable, is more often than not a very secondary presence, frequently partially obscured by the tumble of assembled flowers.

Finally, while we have searched for the simplest and least obtrusive vessels in which to do our professional work, the photographs here testify that we often delight in our own personal collection of odd and unusual containers for our at-home flowers. Understandably, after a long day or week in the shop, we rarely want to labor over our own flowers, so plopping odds and ends into a few choice vases is a perfect solution.

[*Offbeat Containers*]

Flea markets yield bizarre and amusing finds.

The various Ohio potteries such as Roseville, McCoy, and Hall made a wild assortment of shapes throughout the first part of the twentieth century. One of our favorites is a little green squirrel standing at the rim of a cornucopia, which we fill with cuttings from nasturtiums, or lilac flowers (without the leaves), sweet William, columbines, and other small-scale lighthearted flowers. The range of shapes is from deco to disastrous. Some are lofty and some are laughable, but all can be fun to use.

Since we have a passion for old clay pots, we sometimes add a liner and fill them. Pots come in many shapes, sizes, glazes, and textures. A current favorite is a tall, dark red "turpentine catch"—an old, vertically ribbed clay pot that was hung by means of a nail and a wire to catch the sap as it drained through a tube driven into the tree. English and Dutch pots, well known for their imperfect but seductive colors and shapes, both hold field flowers beautifully.

A recent junkyard visit provided us with a faded yellow painted cast-iron vessel shaped like a smelting pot; a square lead pail with a wire handle; an assortment of faded tin maple-syrup pails found in Canada painted blue, red, and yellow; and two large glass battery jars.

Thoughtfully done, an extraordinary container can transform a few ordinary flowers into a poetic event. A handful of tulips, serviceable when plunked into a plain glass jar, becomes extraordinary and special when placed in a vase that shows them to full advantage. And there are economies to be found here as well, for if the flowers and containers are perfectly matched, fewer flowers will fill the bill.

CONDITIONING FLOWERS

[*Chapter 8: There's no magic to it—all conditioning techniques are simply aimed at supporting a flower's ability to refresh itself*]

Internal Conditions

WATER IS A FLOWER'S LIFE-SUPPORT SYSTEM. A cut flower's ability to drink water determines how long that flower will last. A flower's cells work by constantly drawing water up the main stem to the leaves and the flowers, replacing water lost through transpiration. Anything that robs a flower of its water or prevents it from pulling water up into its distribution system will shorten its life. With few exceptions, the single most important act of conditioning is to open up a flower's stem to allow it to take in water freely, and thereafter to keep it open and working. Recutting flower stems after several days and changing a container's water (if possible) help keep this process in good working order.

An equally important task is maintaining the proper water level in all containers. Some flowers drink more voraciously than others, and certain kinds

* Condition flowers in warm
water.
* Put conditioned flowers in a
warm room and in full sunlight or
under a bright light (but not close
enough to burn).
* For flowers that develop inside
a protective sheath, as poppies
do, carefully peel away the outer
layer and gently release the
emerging petals.
* Help tight lilies open by gently
manipulating the closed bud at the
flower tips. Don't force them to
open, coax them a little. See if
slight pressure will help separate
the individual petals.

PREVIOUS PAGES: *Every
membrane of a flower's
surface gives up and takes
in moisture. A big vase of
native daylilies lost out to
an even bigger gust of
wind. Although flowers
fade by mid-evening, new
buds open the next day.*
OPPOSITE: *Lodged in
shallow trays or small pots
for ease of transportation,
farmer's market plants
require constant attention
in the heat of the
afternoon sun.*

of external conditions accelerate water consumption. It takes a stem only a few minutes out of water to scale over and lose its capacity to drink—an eventual death sentence.

External Conditions

Harsh environments put a strain on a flower's system. A flower is composed mostly of water, so exposure to freezing temperatures will cause the water in the surface cells to turn to ice; it expands, bursts the cell tissues, and destroys the flower. During the winter months, it's essential to protect plants and flowers from harsh cold, even for the briefest of times. If the temperature is in the low 40's or below, wrap flowers carefully—even if *you* feel warm enough. Our perception of heat is governed by a number of factors, but a flower knows only the real numbers.

Dry heat is also a problem, and most cut flowers and flowering plants cannot withstand its effects. Dry air acts like a sponge, sucking moisture from a flower's many surfaces, causing it to double and redouble its efforts to refresh its water supply. Any effort to add moisture to the air will improve conditions: a humidifier is ideal, but a pan of water on the radiator or even frequent misting can help.

During the summer months, keep flowers away from drafts created by central air-conditioning systems or individual window units. In fact, avoid keeping flowers in areas that undergo radical temperature changes through the course of a day and night.

Remember that light and warmth hasten the development and activity of a cut flower, whereas cool and dark conditions slow it down. You can make these facts work to your advantage. Prolong the life of flowers by keeping them in cool places away from the sun; get closed flowers to open up faster by putting them in a warm, light place. Since our stone house in the country stays so cool during the week (downright cold in the winter months), flowers we've brought there for a weekend have—often to our astonishment—been perfectly beautiful three weeks later. The cold simply sets them into a sort of limbo. On the other hand, we've seen a flower left on a windowsill in the

blazing summer sun drink all its water in just one day, trying to keep up with the accelerating effects of bright light, intense heat, and dry air.

Mädderlake Conditioning Techniques

1. Cut flower stems decisively with a sharp, clean knife, angling the cut to maximize the surface open to water. The angled cut also allows a stem that might be pressed against a container's bottom surface to keep drinking, rather than becoming blocked.

2. Scrape the sides of the stem for about an inch just above the cut; this helps open up more of the stem's surface to water intake. Discard any bark residue.

3. Split open woody stems or branches by making two or three cuts and crosscuts with a knife or pruning clippers. Scrape away the bark an inch or so up the stem with a knife.

[*Caveat for Misters*]

Some of the more fragile flowers spot if droplets of moisture remain on the petals. Shake the flowers a little to help disperse the droplets, or blot them dry with a paper towel.

4. Return the stems to water immediately after cutting. Some professionals insist on cutting under water. We never have.

5. Remove excess and damaged foliage. Remember that the flower is often farthest away from the water. If all the water goes to support numerous leaves along the way, the flower gets short-changed.

6. Remove all foliage that may fall below water level.

7. As much as possible, allow freshly conditioned flowers to drink water for a while and recompose themselves before you work with them.

8. Always work with clean water and clean containers. Remember to scrub *all* vases, not just the clear ones where the need is obvious.

9. Refresh a container's water as often as possible, taking care to keep all stem ends under water at all times. Just a few minutes out of water and a stem can scale over, preventing water from being taken in. Bacteria develop most quickly in the water of flowers placed in warm and sunny spots. Whenever possible, take a vase of flowers to the sink and change fouled water. Place the arrangement in the sink, with the vase opening directly under the faucet, and flush with fresh, tepid water until all the old water has been forced out. Tip the container slightly to drain a little so that the arrangement can be carried.

10. As individual flowers die, remove spent flowers to keep the arrangement looking fresh *and* to direct energy to the development of emerging buds.

11. For containers that cannot be easily moved, emptied, and refilled, add a thimbleful of bleach to help keep the water clear and to retard the growth of bacteria. Bleach also helps prevent odors from developing, so we always use it with stinky flowers such as allium and fritillaria.

12. When a flower has wilted, or looks a little weak or "iffy," it's often beneficial to shorten the stem length as well as reduce the foliage, thus lessening the distance the water has to travel to refresh the flower. In really bad cases, we assume that the flowers will never completely recover, so we cut the flowers most of the way down and use them in a short vase.

13. Avoid getting water on fuzzy leaves and flowers. They will spot.

OPPOSITE: *A stylish Victorian "frog" happens to hold flowers beautifully, adding a dash of charm in the process.* ABOVE: *The root system of this water hyacinth was so spectacular, we had to find a way to show it.*

[*"Arranging" under Water*]

Since we frequently place large arrangements made for stand-up events on tall pedestals to position the flowers as high as possible, the clear vase is often squarely at eye level. This is a perfect opportunity to play beneath the water's surface and arrange the stems in a beautiful manner. Berries and fruit can contribute to the fun, but if this is your intent, take care not to crowd the vase.

Special Conditioning Techniques

1. Stems and branches that exude a sticky sap must have all fresh cuts cauterized in order to seal in the sap. Immerse stem ends in boiling water for ten to fifteen seconds, or hold them over a candle flame until the end has been sealed. This treatment applies to all poppies, the whole euphorbia family, acanthus, hollyhock, campanula with woody stems, clematis, helleborus, and hydrangea.

2. Some flowers, especially if they've been left out of water for a few hours, benefit from being totally immersed in tepid water, allowing the stems, leaves, and flowers to drink in moisture through their cell walls. Camellias, peonies, roses, lilies, certain orchids, wilted violets, and many other varieties can profit from this practice. In the summer, the two-hour trip to the country with car windows open often takes its toll on the bucket of flowers in the backseat. On arrival, we fill up the bathtub and submerge the neediest in cool water for an hour or two, allowing them to regain their composure. One time, stems of huge, open aureatum lilies that seemed so wilted that we were considering pitching them not only rebounded but felt stronger than ever before.

3. Certain flowers—tulips, for instance—that may have curled up too much can be straightened by carefully wrapping the entire bunch of flowers in wet newspaper to form a straight package. Secure with a rubber band or a piece of tape and submerge under water for an hour or two.

4. Certain flowers that depend on humid conditions—branches of mimosa, for example—should be kept completely wrapped in an air-filled dry cleaner's bag until just before they are to be used. Their delicate clusters of flowers thus remain moist and in perfect condition.

[*Floral Additives*]

Floral additives accomplish three main goals: they provide sugars, which help stimulate growth and development; they add compounds to inhibit the growth of bacteria, thus adding to the stem life of flowers; and they condition the water by adjusting its pH and by precipitating hard solids to the bottom. Additives are available in a variety of formulations. Choose the one geared to your water, or look for a formulation appropriate for all types.

Additives can work a bit like "speed," so measure them carefully. Overstimulating your flowers may shorten their life.

Floral additives are available through most florists. The two largest suppliers are Floralife and Chrysal.

As to the legitimacy or efficacy of the various old-wives'-tale additives—aspirin, pennies, sugar, soda pop, and the like—we have no knowledge or opinion. To the extent that any of these contribute food (sugar, for instance), they are probably doing some good. Though we may not do it, if it works for you, keep at it!

Some flowers hold up out of water. BELOW: *Always start with a clean container. Remove all leaves below water level.* RIGHT: *Billy created this jacket of heather trimmed with mimosas, leptospermum, and nerine lilies for a fashionable New York store opening.*

[*Getting the Most Life Out of Your Flowers*]

• Keep them cool and away from excessive heat and light.

• Keep them moist and away from dry air and drafts.

• Recut the stems as often as possible.

• Change the water as soon as it begins to appear cloudy.

• Use a floral additive as a nutrient source and a water conditioner.

• Pick spent flowers off of flowers with multiple blooms to encourage new buds to open.

• Keep foliage to a minimum to direct the stem's energy into the flowers themselves.

[*Chapter 9: Why we choose the flowers we choose,*
and why we arrange them the way we do]

CONSIDERATIONS OF STYLE

WE ARE NEVER SHOOTING IN THE DARK. Over the years, as
we've struggled to learn our business, we've developed a set of criteria about
why we do what we do, and we find that we're pretty consistent within our
choices. In other words, we now know what using fresh flowers represents to
us, and this knowledge governs our actions.

It's helpful to understand the parameters of the style or styles that appeal to
you so that you can measure and evaluate your future decisions by something
other than instinct or luck. If you don't understand why you're doing something, you won't really know how to go about doing it. True, you may be
able to replicate someone else's style or to approximate something you've seen
or learned, but you'll never really be able to make something new and perfectly appropriate unless you've taken the time to reason out what you're trying to accomplish with your efforts. There are four distinct approaches to
choosing and working with flowers.

ABOVE: *A decidedly Dutch mix combines wildly different flowers in an energetic, exuberant tangle.* OPPOSITE: *A typically English arrangement brings the nearby woods and fields into the living room.*

PREVIOUS PAGES: *Choose flowers appropriate to the intended setting. Isn't it remarkable that just two stems of lilies can stand up to a room as grand as this one in Stoneleigh Abbey? Down the hall, a spectacular array of hybrid sweet peas presides over the Royal bed.*

Flowers that Re-create Past Styles

Throughout history, certain styles of arranging have evolved that can be observed, studied, and emulated.

THE FLEMISH STYLE. These elaborate arrangements of unexpected natural elements, asymmetrically mixed and exuberantly arranged, were probably composed mostly on canvas. They are often illogical, brimming with flowers drawn from different seasons and growing regions. Exotic tulip varieties, swollen poppies, acanthus, rare garden flowers, wildflowers, and branches laden with ripening fruit—from pomegranate to pears to quince—are combined with butterflies, bizarre insects, and other botanical delights in the paintings of Jan van Eyck, Jan van Huysum, Jan Van Os, Jacob von Walscappelle, and many others. The essence of the Flemish style lies almost wholly in the wild and unrestrained choice of ingredients, not so much in the way in which they are combined.

THE FRENCH STYLE. A canvass of the best flower shops in Paris today will reveal a similar style of arranging in many of them: low mounds of flowers placed or tucked cheek-to-jowl, sometimes in concentric circles, other times more randomly mixed, but generally symmetrical and packed to the gills like giant nosegays. Larger arrangements are symmetrically disposed as well, the flowers seeming to emanate from a central point and fanning out equally in all directions but down. In contrast to the Flemish style, the French style is defined by the method in which the flowers are combined and assembled, not by the particular choice of flowers.

THE JAPANESE STYLE. Although I know little about it, the famous Japanese practice of ikebana is a story in itself, whose meanings and methods often transcend mere arranging. Ikebana has never held much fascination for us at Pure Mädderlake, for it seems to be too much about learning conditions and rules and therefore about something other than simply working with beautiful flowers. The object of arranging in the practice of ikebana seems to be to evoke an idealized world, or to mirror or present again ideas that have been formed about the natural world. Its rules and laws and forms have been passed down through countless generations of practitioners. Although those who practice the true art of ikebana may create stylish configurations using a minimal flower palette, the Japanese style has begot many meager imitators who, knowing little of the great tradition, seem to be satisfied with combining two or three exotic elements into what we feel are, most often, decidedly unattractive and uncomfortable concoctions.

THE ENGLISH STYLE. It might be easiest to picture this style by remembering that the purpose of arranging in this manner is to gather the various flowers found in English perennial borders and nearby fields, and then loosely assemble them in a pot or a jar, much as they were growing outdoors. This kind of idiosyncratic, herbaceous melange might be described as literally bringing the garden indoors.

Of the four groups, the French and Japanese styles are more studied and "stylish." The manner in which the flowers are arranged is as evident in the final assemblage as are the flowers. By contrast, the English and Flemish styles produce less arranged-looking results that rely first and foremost on the appearance of the material, *not* on the way in which it has been combined.

Learn to be observant and to be original with what you see, not just to imitate. Any or all of the above can be jumping-off points for your own ideas.

Flowers as Heralds of High Style

This distinctive point of view often produces somewhat mannered results. We sense that the flowers of high style are not meant to evoke images of the world around us, but to transport us out of our world by bringing an exotic, otherworldly presence to their setting, suggesting that they are from another realm or place—a Moorish palace, perhaps, a summer villa on the Bosporus, or a remote Indian retreat.

High-style flowers are generally chosen for their elegance of line and silhouette and their clarity or simplicity of color. They are often white: long, arching stems of phalaenopsis orchids; clouds of 'Casablanca lilies'; cascades of long dendrobium orchids; languid stems of powder-white calla lily flowers; erotic cream-colored anthuriums tinged with green edges—all make up the stable of high-style flowers.

[*Flowers as Obligation*]

Far too often, flowers are bought and used out of a sense that they are a requirement to be provided rather than a presence to be delivered. Middle-of-the-road restaurants are a prime offender in this category, placing a half-dead rose or a dime's worth of statice or yarrow on the table, which simply causes the setting to look dreary and bedraggled. It's better to spend your money elsewhere than to buy flowers because you feel that you ought to have them.

Sexy, sensuous stems of eremerus, **LEFT**, belong to the stable of high-style flowers, as do the auratum and Casablanca lilies used in the powerhouse arrangement, **ABOVE**. **BELOW**: Equally tailored to its decor, the mantel flowers at the Magnolia Inn in Savannah—spirea, Queen Anne's lace, azaleas, and geraniums—reprise the values, textures, and colors in the floral frieze and the stippled walls. **OPPOSITE**: A salad mix of green dill, mallow flowers, columbine, and loosestrife blends quietly into the serenity of its setting.

Cut from around our country house, one of our three surviving wild lilies works to upstage a more "ordinary" yellow lily in this all natural gathering of miniature double clematis and blue salvia flowers. Natural flower arrangements are mostly just about the flowers themselves.

The arrangements are sometimes aggressively overscaled, and the flowers are often sparsely arrayed in elegant, expensive-looking containers or massed out in large glass globes or urns.

High-style flowers are power flowers, flowers that comport themselves in such a way as to look and feel expensive and important.

Flowers as Decor

In this approach, flowers are chosen to be consistent with the way their setting has been decorated—that is to say, the flowers, like the curtains, fabrics, and other furnishing elements, become part of a carefully regulated aesthetic scheme, each piece carefully coordinated to each other piece, so that, together, they form a consistent and unbroken gestalt. Those who use flowers in this manner seem to hold that fresh flowers are chosen to blend in and add to the overall "look" of the room. The flowers are not meant to be remarkable in and of themselves, but simply to contribute to the decor.

Whereas this is certainly an understandable and serviceable approach to using flowers, more often than not for us it borders on predictability and produces unexciting and sometimes even negligible results. Arrangements of silk flowers are the ultimate "decor" solutions.

Flowers as Reflections of Nature

This view holds that the best flowers are first and foremost messengers of the natural world, imbued with the inherent power to remind us by their simple presence of the larger natural world.

Flowers that are able to fulfill this promise are chosen primarily for how beautiful they are as individual flowers. Not all flowers fill this bill, for many have been bred and grown for other reasons and little resemble their more capable counterparts. **SELECTING APPROPRIATE FLOWERS IS THE SINGLE MOST IMPORTANT STEP** in the practice of using flowers as elements of nature.

Natural flowers fit into any kind of setting without the restriction of having to conform to it. In fact, natural flowers are often chosen and positioned to contrast with their setting in order to stand apart from it and carry their message unhindered by their surroundings. Their very purpose is to engage our attention and remind us of the world outside, to transport us, if even for a moment, to something bigger and more eternal.

They can be arranged in simple or in complex ways, as long as the method of arranging does not dominate or subjugate the material itself.

It is in this comfortable little domain, peppered with shades and shards of some of the flowers of history, that we heartily feel we belong, and this knowledge always shapes and guides our choices of flowers and the ways in which we assemble them.

Before you begin, try to understand the general framework of your efforts and the goals you want to achieve. The more you know, the better you will be and the easier your choices will become.

At a country place near Beaune, a big branch of lilac is casually stuck in a vase with bearded iris and tall stems of cow parsley.

[Chapter 10: On scale, color, texture,

form, shape, and space]

BUILDING BLOCKS

TO FASHION AN ORIGINAL ARRANGEMENT of flowers, you will inevitably be called upon to consider and evaluate choices within the following categories. Arrangers unfamiliar with these issues should tackle them and sort them out until you develop an understanding of the various principles and relationships at work. Doing this will make your future work much easier and, I think, better and more varied. Don't be discouraged if it seems more obvious for some. Some people are born with an innate feel for all this, even if they don't quite understand or can't verbalize the underlying reasons for their decisions.

SCALE. Questions of scale within an arrangement concern the degree of contrast you elect to make between the various individual flowers. A mix of flowers of similar scales is vastly different in appearance and presence from an arrangement of flowers of disparate scales, the latter generally louder than the former.

Questions of scale will also arise when you're making a relationship between the bulk of the arrangement and the container. Do the flowers overwhelm and overpower the container, make a sort of normal-feeling relationship with it, or cower in its presence? These ideas will become apparent to you as you work with and consider them. Understanding the drama of scale considerations will allow you to exaggerate or understate your work to various effects, as well as work in the "normal" range.

Finally, the scale of the whole work must be considered with regard to its ultimate setting. Will it shout, talk, or whisper in the room in which it is going? The scale of the whole arrangement to the volume of the room will practically guarantee its resulting voice.

COLOR. Considerations within the realm of color run from monochromatic to spectral and everything in between. The number of different colors used and the degree of contrast between them greatly affect the action of the mix. The more harmonious and closer in value the choices are, the quieter the result will be; the more the colors clash or energize each other, the louder it all gets.

As with notions of scale, the color of the arrangement needs to be considered with an eye to the setting. Will it blend in or stand out?

TEXTURE. Different flowers have different forms and values. Some are hard, some are soft; some are linear, others are concentric. Mixing dissimilar textures usually achieves more striking or more dramatic results, while putting similar values side by side usually produces a gentler harmony.

FORM. The poles of form are symmetry and asymmetry. Certain kinds of arrangements are composed to be symmetrical about a center axis, or center point, while others are balanced in more complex ways. One achieves its final harmony in a static way; the other, dynamic.

SHAPE. Decisions about form affect overall shape. The shape or outline of an arrangement can be regular—that is, falling within some sort of geometric figure—or jagged and irregular.

SPACE. The space of an arrangement is the interior zone that is contained by the outer shape. Certain arranging techniques "fill up" or eliminate the inner space, while others preserve it and use it.

PREVIOUS PAGES: *The first several moves in a natural mix are usually the boldest. Here, for starters, we paired a branch of charentais melon with a flowering stalk of zucchini. Usually tall and leggy, Peruvian lilies were cut down to nestle next to geranium flowers in a painted tole cup.*

Perhaps because Billy was trained in graphic design and I studied architecture, space, shape, and form are the elements of flower arranging that most intrigue us, so let's start there. Three basic shapes govern the symmetrical series: a circle (with its subset, a fan), a rectangle (with its subset, a square), and a triangle. Symmetry demands equal and opposite choices to achieve its particular equation of balance. Certain flower arrangers are slaves to these forms, forcing their flowers to fit into perfect invisible geometric figures, or to follow linear configurations such as the classic diagonal line or "S" curve.

French bouquets are often perfectly symmetrical around their center point, and many large arrangements such as formal hotel work are achieved by inserting the same number of the same kinds of flowers evenly spaced throughout the composition, whether done in a relatively frontal or a more three-dimensional fashion.

Many arrangers—especially those who have studied arranging techniques—seem to subscribe to the notion that a flower arrangement is as much a "display" as anything else, and they design it to be seen most advantageously from one point. It almost always has a back and a front, with the flowers assiduously placed facing out. Flowers made in this manner often appear self-conscious to us, as if the technique of arranging them were more important than the beauty of the various flowers themselves. We are far more interested in asymmetry than symmetry, and our work reflects that bias.

Asymmetrical arranging arrives at its peculiar or individual sense of harmony by countering one kind of move with an opposing move of equal strength or value but different character—a sort of parry and thrust, parry and thrust routine. When we arrange, we generally rotate the container after placing each flower to keep an eye on the whole composition and avoid producing a lopsided or one-sided result. The process of arranging, then, becomes a series of moves and countermoves that constantly alter the balance of the mix until an appropriate result is achieved. Generally speaking, the first few choices dramatically throw the arrangement off one way or the other, but gradually the kinds of changes become smaller and smaller until the final few flowers to be added don't affect the overall balance but simply provide grace notes, little finishing touches.

Visual drama can be balanced in many different ways: a diverse range of colors, scales, and flower types produces an action-packed mix; full-blown Casablanca lilies and leggy salvia bed down together in an equally dramatic but quieter way.

When we looked at the back of the flowers made for our room at the Mt. Kenya Safari Club, we found the "back" . . . and nothing but the back. Flowers made in this fashion are more of a stiff "display" than an arrangement.

The choice of working toward a dynamic rather than a static solution practically dictates that the overall shape or outline of the arrangement will not only be irregular but, depending on which side it's viewed from, will look unique from all different angles. The amount of irregularity can be controlled, of course, but we often like very haphazard silhouettes.

With a few exceptions perhaps, we almost always try to retain some inner space within our arrangements rather than clogging them up. Many arrangers stuff their mixes with flowers, but we consciously fight to keep from choking the interior space, preserving a sense of transparency by working with a lighter number of ingredients and by removing a great deal of excess greenery before a flower is used. Generally, the flowering materials we've chosen are interesting in and of themselves and demand to be seen as individual pieces rather than completely sacrificed to blend into an overall haze. The larger the project, the harder it is to achieve this transparency, yet a sense of depth and visual penetration can always be alluded to, if not actually provided.

In order to activate the inner space, that is to say, to prevent it from simply becoming residual or leftover, we almost always cut some of the flowers that will ultimately define the outer edge short and insert them into the center of the mix. The observer's eye registers the connection and feels the positive value of that inner point to the whole. The opposite way of arranging leaves the center to fend for itself (that is to say, to die) and extends or propels all the flowers equally to the outer edges. We see arrangements such as this as exploding works, with all the flowers fanned out from a center point, en route to outer space.

We answer questions of texture and scale based both on what is available and most interesting to use, and then on how these choices can support our goals. If the best available materials are similar in scale, we find a way to push them by how we assemble them. Although we generally prefer combining vastly different textural and scale values rather than making mixes of very similar flowers, there is certainly a time and a place for the latter. Since we'll often begin an arrangement with a structure or skeleton of branches or other linear elements, this almost always ensures that the final result will have a range of hard and soft ingredients and therefore a dramatic textural mix.

Flowers tough enough to share a room with a Lichtenstein painting nee strong shapes and clear, vibrant colors—like the eremerus, hybrid delphini um, and nursery-grown garden lilies we used, **RIGHT**, at Washington's National Gallery of Art. **BELOW**: A quiet cluster of similar flower values leaves most of the drama to the jazzy container.

A big jump in scale in the flower choices and a mix of hard and soft textures, like those ABOVE, *virtually guarantee a loud "look-at-me" kind of mix.* OPPO-SITE: *By contrast, this summer concoction of soft garden flowers, a mix of nasturtiums, coreopsis, rudbeckia, potentilla, and clusters of robin hood roses gains its voice from a razzle-dazzle mix of electric colors.*

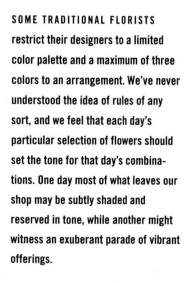

SOME TRADITIONAL FLORISTS restrict their designers to a limited color palette and a maximum of three colors to an arrangement. We've never understood the idea of rules of any sort, and we feel that each day's particular selection of flowers should set the tone for that day's combinations. One day most of what leaves our shop may be subtly shaded and reserved in tone, while another might witness an exuberant parade of vibrant offerings.

Finally, as far as we're concerned, color is a completely subjective topic. We don't believe that there are certain colors that can't or shouldn't be used together, as many proclaim. Because the actual color of a flower is such a complex value, it's not enough to say that it is red, or it is blue, since there are so many values of each one. One red might make an orange look dreary, while another red might give it a lift and make it seem bright and chipper.

Colors can't be outlawed by name alone, only by what effect they actually provoke in the other colors they are to join. We all know that certain colors vibrate when placed next to certain others, creating a third color in the process. Other colors when placed side by side harmonize so effectively that they appear to be perfectly at rest.

It should be noted, too, that some colors have associative values and might bring that value to the arrangement. All-white arrangements might seem weddinglike to some, funereal to others. Then again, some call pink flowers feminine; blue, masculine; red, whorish; orange, tropical; and so forth.

When all is said and done, **THERE ARE NO RIGHT OR WRONG CHOICES**, only consequences. But the more completely you understand the principles underlying the creative act, whether intuitively or through careful thought and reasoning, the better your work will be. Of that we're absolutely sure.

TWO COLOR TRAITS dominate standard production flowers: sharp and clear, and flat and dull.

The two lilies most often found in bucket shops are piercing orange and sharp yellow; iris colors are usually clear tones of blue and yellow; liatris is a strident purple; daisies are pure white; carnations are often dead red and dead white; gerbera daisies—looking dyed, although they're not—come in a whole range of vivid-but-shocking clear color values, while the ubiquitous selection of mums ranges from dull mauve and pale pink through a wan, lemon-yellow to a dishwater brown—all looking as if some of the color had been drained out of the flower, leaving a pale residue. Although these flowers typically constitute the stable of choices for mixed arrangements, none combines well with others, for each color has so little to do with any other. By contrast, flowers with complex tonalities and rich hues and shadings—garden roses are a prime example—harmonize far more readily into a mix of dissimilar flowers.

Flower colors should not look as if they've been bred to be the least objectionable choices. To the contrary, they should exhibit exciting qualities such as nuance, shading, depth, and complexity. You should be able to look at a flower and think, "Now *that's* really a gorgeous color."

Pumpkin lilies shade from their namesake color to caramel and creamy tones; the campanula family offers blue flowers in many borderline hues ranging from purple, deep ink, and evening shade colors, all the way to soft, powder-blue daylight tones. Some of the most beautiful roses ramble through a gamut of creamy whites, shading from pale peach to sunset yellows; peonies range from soft white to a sensuous coral color, touching on a dozen pinks and reds in between.

Complex colors combine well because their tones overlap when placed side by side. A yellow that contains some red and some orange blends well with a variety of red and orange colors, and resonates favorably with a range of blues that have similar or opposing overtones. By contrast, a pure, dead yellow has no complex tonal makeup and sits alone and mute alongside other colors.

STEP BY STEP

GIVE YOURSELF PLENTY OF ROOM for your efforts. There's nothing worse than falling all over your materials or not being able to easily see what you have to work with as you're working.

Condition flowers and clean off excess leaves and side stems; prune out branches and branched flowers to clean, pretty shapes. Survey the results.

The flowers you've chosen should be suggesting both the containers they would look best in and the best ways in which they might be combined. A little mental work before you actually begin will simplify your later efforts.

Once you've chosen a container, devise the means by which the flowers are going to be held in place. A good shapely branch or two carefully lodged in place is a great start, for it helps hold all other flowers where you put them. The more complex the underwater branching, the better, for it will allow you to lock flowers into place. Or cross and crisscross the first five or six stems

PREVIOUS PAGES: *Give yourself a good, strong start. A carefully wedged fig branch in this iron-stone soup tureen forms an anchor for the roses and gladiolas to follow. Gladiola flowers were cut into thirds and used as individual flowers, not long stems. Look at the difference.*

as you insert them to fashion a sturdy web in which future flowers will be anchored. If you're desperate, pierce a thick stem with a knife and thread another stem through it. Once you understand the importance of this first step, you'll discover dozens of ways to use various flowers to this purpose.

Begin with the strongest, most important flowers and work toward the more ephemeral ones. Check through your flower shapes and select the one or two that will tumble over the edge of the container and give the arrangement a comfortable feeling. It's easy to find the flowers that will carry the top of the arrangement, but it's much more difficult to find the ones to fashion a beautiful bottom edge. Flowers with curvy stems—anemones, tulips, ranunculus, poppies—sport shapes that will nestle over the rim of a vase. In fact, a beautifully arched tulip with a lush, green leaf is a perfect first flower. Cut the stem so that the leaf just drapes over the edge of the container.

LEFT, ABOVE, AND OPPOSITE: *On the outskirts of Lucca, we found an unusual gray-green palette to work with. Beginning with fruited olive branches, we added the last dregs cut from a nearby hydrangea bush, then tall plump sage and basil cut from the herb garden, and finished this airy mix with scabiosa, trumpet vine, rose-of-sharon, and a branch from a pomegranate bush.*

• A good, sharp, clean knife—one that folds so that you can slip it in your pocket and keep it with you

• A good pair of heavy-duty clippers, such as Felco

• A thorn stripper for dethorning rose stems painlessly (if you use a lot of garden roses)

• Floral foam

• Thin (³⁄₁₆-inch) waterproof green tape for securing foam brick into a dish

• Green wire for fastening jobs that won't show

• Wire cutters

• Water tubes for the times when you need to add flowers to the perimeter of an arrangement and the stems can't possibly reach the water in the container

Don't overlook the vegetable garden! Start with something sturdy and structural—like a branch of grapes, LEFT. Then, OPPOSITE, add green tomatoes, white symphoracarpa berries, Virginia creeper, phlox, and a rose or two.

Rotate the vase as you work and keep looking at the whole composition. Each time a new flower is added, it will jostle the other flowers, so check and readjust flowers as necessary.

Sketch in the important parts of the arrangement so that you quickly establish a sense of its mass and outer shape. Consider how each flower is changing the balance as you work, and evaluate how much more you need to add before the arrangement is complete. Remember that many flowers will open up and grow in size as they develop—so leave plenty of room for this process. A lily bloom needs twice as much room for its open flower than for its bud. Remember, too, that tulips actually elongate as they develop, so factor this into the equation as well.

LEARN WHEN TO STOP. This takes practice, but at one point or another, you should feel perfectly satisfied with what you have made. This means that you're done.

[Frogs]

A frog is any device that is added to a container to help secure the flowers. The most ubiquitous frog is a heavy green metal disk with concentric rings of pointed spikes. This is generally attached to the bottom of a shallow bowl with floral tape.

We seldom use frogs, for they tend to present the flowers they hold in a very stylized relationship to the container, but antique frogs are often amusing. One we love is a ceramic toad with holes in its back; another, a bird's nest with pale blue eggs—both perfect for frivolous concoctions. Keep your eye out at flea markets for a strange assortment of possibilities.

When a single container is not big enough to support a large arrangement, there are various tricks to getting the job done.

Grand arrangements such as those at New York's Metropolitan Museum are made in special three-tiered containers that allow flowers to be positioned far above the main level. Thus lilies and roses whose stems are only two feet long can appear seven to eight feet above the bottom of the arrangement. Large branches and other big greens sketch in the bulk of the composition, and a succession of flowers is placed in all three levels.

When the container itself cannot be extended, flowers can be fitted with water tubes and carefully secured in the outer areas of the arrangement. This technique works best when the arrangement has an intricate structure of branches and other sturdy flowers in which to lodge them, and is useful mostly for special-event flowers, for the tubes contain only enough water to supply a flower for half a day or so.

A third method involves making one flower composition that spans several different containers, allowing the flowers to be easily extended laterally if not vertically. This solution is particularly successful when the two or three vases are different heights and shapes. A twenty-four-inch-tall glass rectangle placed near an eighteen-inch-cylinder and a fifteen-inch-square makes a great setting for a tumble of branches and flowers.

Select a shallow bowl of a size suitable for your purposes—the shorter the sides the better, for you will want to lodge flowers so that they drape down to the table surface.

Hold the block of oasis over the container and determine the size you will need, cut the block, and wedge it firmly into place. You may need to shave the sides of the block to match the slant of the bowl. If the container needs more than one block, wedge them side by side.

Take thin green tape and cross and crisscross the block, adhering the tape firmly to the container.

Lay down a layer of tape along the perimeter of the container to reinforce the tape's holding power, and trim excess below the rim.

Move the container to the sink and let the brick absorb tepid water until it is completely full (and stops bubbling); or mix a solution of floral additive and water in the sink or in a large bucket and submerge until full.

Once the brick is thoroughly soaked, place the container on an elevated base (a low mixing bowl or an upside-down flowerpot) so that you can fill in the lower edges more easily.

Search your material carefully for what value each particular piece has to offer, then sketch in the high and low points early on. We began with shapely hawthorn branches, then added rugosa roses, peonies, and columbines. Finally —like pinning on a dazzling brooch—we punctuated the whole thing with a big juicy clematis.

PREVIOUS PAGE: *In deference to the spectacular ancient leather wallpaper behind and the striking vessel below, a spare cluster of French stock, delphinium, and rhododendron is all that is called for here.* THIS PAGE: *Especially in the most elegant of settings, we long for a reminder of the woods and wilds. This lavish tangle of barberry, rhododendron, spirea, stock, and lillies—mostly clipped from the castle grounds—transports the wild outdoors indoors in a lively and stately fashion.*

Powerhouse flowers, like these Casablanca lilies, are hard to combine but incredible by themselves. Unless you are really afraid of staining, leave the pollen on the anthers. The stark white flower is far more beautiful with fuzzy rust-colored centers intact.

• Use a flower's foliage, not extraneous greens, to add depth and set off the individual blooms.
• Arrange flowers assymetrically to maintain a natural feeling.
• Keep it simple—the straightforward pewter holder anchors the tangle of stems and leaves and reinforces the visual strength of the whole.

A vibrant mass of rhododendron flowers creates a dazzling sunlit flower jewel. Many landscape flowers are but distant dots of color. Bringing them closer reveals a delicate beauty we rarely see in their natural setting.

• These flowers gain their visual pizzazz from being gathered tightly together.
• While sharp variations in colors produce dramatic contrasts, subtle variations resonate in a delicate and delicious fashion.

An odd assortment of greenhouse cuttings—
a stem of euphorbia, a branch of jasmine, and
a bergenia flower—combine in a surprising
and harmonious way.

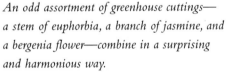

◆ Look for flowers in all sorts of places, and
don't reject anything until you have given it
some careful consideration.
◆ Keep arrangements looking fresh; as flowers
fade, pick the old ones off.
◆ Cuttings casually tucked into a container
rather than carefully arranged speak mostly
about the individual qualities of the flowers
themselves, not the "art" of the arranger.

A shiny porcelain milk pitcher holds an array
of greenhouse, garden, woodland, and field
flowers: shapely black dragon lilies, currant
branches, phlox, mustard, bergenia, geraniums, and begonias.

◆ A variety of textures and flower shapes is
one way to bring life to an arrangement; while
some traditional mixes may seem bland and
quiet, this exuberant set of choices feels downright feisty.
◆ While stark white lilies would have stuck
out of this arrangement, the subtle shadings
and softer shape of these trumpet lilies manage to bob and weave in and out of the mix
and feel a part of the whole.

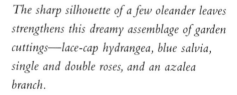

The sharp silhouette of a few oleander leaves strengthens this dreamy assemblage of garden cuttings—lace-cap hydrangea, blue salvia, single and double roses, and an azalea branch.

♦ *Cut out unwanted foliage, but leave undamaged leaves when they can add a presence to the mix; the fewer the flowers used, the more important the greenery becomes.*

♦ *Let one choice lead to another—the pale single rose looked good next to the double whites; the white roses suggested the oleander with its rosettes of pink flowers; they in turn led to the pink azalea; and so forth.*

♦ *When the individual flowers you have chosen are really beautiful, leave plenty of space around them so that they can be properly seen.*

♦ *Don't overdo; the sparseness of this arrangement allows the strength of certain flowers and leaves to play nicely against the delicacy of others.*

A profusion of midsummer flowers stuffed into an enamelled metal pitcher bring the overloaded garden right onto the table. Raspberry branches sporting fruit form a nest for cosmos, coreopsis, trumpet vine, campanula, veronica, and a blood red zinnia.

♦ *Raid the vegetable garden for fruits and flowers.*

♦ *The natural surroundings often suggest ways to combine flowers. Our own gardens are anything but neat and tidy, so our flower mixes often end up wild and energetic.*

♦ *Think of the setting when choosing the flowers. Since this arrangement was made for a late night affair, we chose lighter flowers to pick up and reflect the lantern light. A dark arrangement would have been lost.*

A rough and tumble mix from a variety of sources illustrates the seemingly limitless range of floral possibilities available to those who care to look.

• Cut from greenhouse plants—at 11 o'clock, hot pink mandevilla vine flowers; at 3:00 and at 7:30, geraniums; at 8:00, pale blue plumbago; at 6:00, a tumble of exotic purple-blue blooms cut from a rain forest vine called thunbergia.

• Cut from the garden—at 9:00 and 12:00, spirea thunbergia; at 2:30, fritellaria imperialis; near 9:00, a poppy.

• Found at the tropical flower store in the market—at 1:00, red cockscomb; at 11:00, bulbanella (a flower new to us); spiky yellow chamanaethus sits smack in the center of the mix.

A jumble of columbine, snowballs, mock orange, bearded iris, and painted daisies is wild and energetic.

• Loose and leggy flowers look wild to our eyes, while compact flowers appear more cultivated.

• Though a natural arrangement should look a little messy, remove spent flowers when they detract from the mix. A bearded iris may produce as many as five flowers through the life of the arrangement; pick off the remains if they offend.

• Water pitchers come in an infinite variety of shapes and finishes and are perfect for holding fistfuls of flowers. Check out local tag sales and flea markets to add to your collection of possibilities.

For an event honoring the Hotchkiss School, we fashioned blue and white flowers (the school colors) in trophy bowls. Elegant roses or lilies would have looked pretty but unconnected to the evening's participants.

❧ Sometimes the lushness of an arrangement is created strictly by the opulence of the flowers; other times, when the greenery is especially fresh looking and appealing, use the green branches as "flowers."

An elegant silver water pitcher borrowed from a Holland pantry holds lilac, canterbury bells, and sweet peas.

❧ Learn to vary your flower combinations through the many possibilities. Here, while the textures and shapes of the flowers are dramatically different, the color shadings are extremely subtle.

❧ Look for the flowers that will break the edge of the vase; this creates a more relaxed, more comfortable appearance.

❧ Remember to burn the stem ends of canterbury bells.

❧ Keep interior foliage to a minimum to give flowers "breathing room."

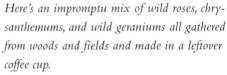

Here's an impromptu mix of wild roses, chry-santhemums, and wild geraniums all gathered from woods and fields and made in a leftover coffee cup.

• *A really beautiful mix of flowers never depends on its container; you can fashion flowers in anything.*

• *Although there are some flowers that do not hold when cut, the myth that most wildflow-ers do not last is just that.*

• *Cut early in the day or in the cool of the evening—never in the heat of the afternoon sun.*

• *Refresh wilted flowers by totally submerg-ing them in cool water for an hour or two.*

• *Leave rare and endangered species growing for everyone to enjoy.*

An old glazed inkwell holds snips of bladder-wort, wild rose, and wood hyacinth.

• *Learn to watch and appreciate the entire life of a flower or an arrangement. We are so geared to having everything at its peak that we miss the beauty of flowers that fade gracefully.*

• *There are many places in the house for tiny flowers: a bathroom sink, a kitchen sill, a bedside table, or a dinner table set for two.*

• *Keep a variety of small containers handy for flowers pinched off of plants or out of the garden, or for broken bits or discards from a larger arranging project.*

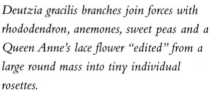

Deutzia gracilis branches join forces with rhododendron, anemones, sweet peas and a Queen Anne's lace flower "edited" from a large round mass into tiny individual rosettes.

❧ *Learn to rework flowers to your purposes; many cluster flowers of regular shape (hydrangea is a perfect example) can be reshaped by eliminating part of the mass of the flower.*

❧ *Change linear flowers such as gladiolus, euphorbia fulgens, freesia, and campanula by plucking individual flowers out of the line. Don't hesitate to adjust flowers to fit your needs.*

❧ *As we did in this antique cocoa tin, tuck a liner into any nonwatertight container to press it into service.*

Somewhat languid wood hyacinths found growing in the shade of a tree pleasantly soften a mix of sweet peas and narcissus.

❧ *Often, the least attractive branches and flowers in a natural setting make the best arranging choices; leggy and straggly flowers often sport interesting shapes.*

❧ *While these wood hyacinths, stretched to the limits in search of light, looked a little droopy under the tree, the resulting curves provided us with a positive counterpoint to the more upright sweet peas and narcissus.*

❧ *Move flowers around. This windowsill near a writing desk in an English country house made a perfect daytime backdrop for this sweet mix; at night, we moved them onto a table under the lamplight.*

❧ *Avoid stiff flowers. Keep your choices and combinations personal looking and animated.*

A daddy longlegs drinks nectar from a yellow nerine lily in this strange but lively mix of local weeds and imported tropical flowers.

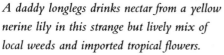 *Keep reaching for new combinations—you have nothing to lose and everything to gain. Those who reduce flowers to a predictable set of choices and combinations reduce flowers to a commodity status and deny the qualities that make raw nature so intriguing and so incredibly appealing.*

Always be on the lookout for new color mixes. Familiar colors look fresh when juxtaposed with off-beat neighbors. Here, several shades of purple-blue set off odd combinations of yellows and pinks and produce a surprisingly interesting result in which each color looks new and noticeable.

A sinkside assortment of intensely toned poppies brightens some of the drudgery of kitchen work.

Poppies are among the flowers that exude a milky sap when cut and therefore require a seared or burnt stem-end to last.

Encourage stubborn flowers to open by gently cracking tight buds with thumb and forefinger.

The beauty of certain flowers lies in their ability to change and develop over the course of their brief lives. Poppies are among the most dramatic, beginning as tight furry buds, splitting open and unfurling to form fragile paper fans, and finally dropping their delicate petals, leaving only their fuzzy centers behind.

FLOWERS FOR THE TABLE

IT'S HARD TO IGNORE FLOWERS smack-dab in the middle of the table. If they're ugly or uninspired, you still have to look at them for the duration of the meal. But if they're glorious … well, that's another story.

More often than not, flowers contribute a subtle and peripheral presence to their surroundings. Table flowers, however, are made to be center stage, the star of the show, holding the guests hostage until the last drop has been quaffed and the chairs pushed away from the table. They provide handy visual refuge from an undesirable dinner partner, a potential at-hand topic if the conversation takes a turn in the wrong direction, or a simple source of visual delight throughout the evening.

We reason, then, that of all the different kinds of flowers you can make, table flowers should be especially beautiful—fascinating, surprising even, intriguing to gaze upon.

PREVIOUS PAGES: *A simple combination of forget-me-nots, campanula, and yellow narcissus grace a lunch table in a Utrecht café. A handful of snowy-white thalia daffodils have that fresh, just-picked look.* BELOW: *Four fall berries—callicarpa, cotoneaster, symphoracarpa, and bayberry—combine with variegated daphne leaves, eunoymous branches, and a handful of tiny, bright flowers to make a spectacular fall centerpeice.* OPPOSITE: *A lighthearted spring ensemble includes checkerboard lilies, grape hyacinths, miniature narcissus, and a knot of field violets.*

Of course, there are plenty of times when the flowers planned for the middle of the table needn't be aggressively made, and a simple choice fits the bill perfectly. They should then be carefully chosen to be as lovely in their simplicity as can possibly be found. When simplicity is the order of the day, the result needn't be dull or unremarkable.

After learning that a certain charity event, even though it was being held in the grand gilded ballroom of New York's famous Plaza Hotel, was being billed as a low-key "Sunday Supper," with a menu of chicken pot pies, simple green salad, and carafes of white wine, we felt that the flowers we were asked to provide ought to actively support the theme of the evening. Our goal was to make whatever we would do look and feel as if a few of the ladies had gotten together and done it themselves, and not to seem as if a fancy florist had waltzed in and provided the goods.

[*Alice Waters*]

I guess that I think about flowers much the way I do about food. They are both about freshness, aroma, texture, color, most important seasonality, and even flavor. At Chez Panisse, we feel that they work together to reinforce these concerns. The food displays that we have at the restaurant provide visual tableaus reflecting our passion for ingredients, while the flower arrangements that we have, by far the most dramatic visual element in the restaurant, are essentially just more exotic living sculptural expressions of the same spirit.

While I don't like flowers on the table itself (except perhaps for a small bouquet of violets), they have always had an important presence in the dining rooms. I find myself looking forward to the flowers as much as the food. Fall leaves fill the restaurant in September (liquid ambar, maples on fire, copper beech). I love big informal arrangements that seem to fill the room with a feeling of the outdoors. Winter brings bare branches of beautiful shapes like birch, rose hips, and willow.

Spring enchants me with its lime green and white parrot tulips and the maroon tulips that remind me so much of the striated radicchio lettuces in the kitchen. Having them mixed in with flowering almonds, magnolias, cherry and plum blossoms provides a hint of the summer fruits to follow. Summer fills the dining room with garden roses, boughs of Bank's roses, and later the deep Tuscany rose, which is my favorite. These arrangements are always short-lived, as fragile as very ripe, but perishable produce. Probably the most appealing flower itself to me is the trailing nasturtium of earthy yellows, and deep oranges and reds, a charming and edible tribute to summer's waning moments.

Alice Waters is the owner of Chez Panisse in Berkeley, California.

OPPOSITE: *The more spectacular the flowers, the fewer you need to show. More roses here would have been overkill.* RIGHT: *Lots of tender spring flowers, including an errant spray of bleeding heart, combine in an airy mix.*

We asked our friends at Wolfman-Gold & Good Company, a wonderful SoHo shop that specializes in white tableware of all sorts and styles, to lend us an odd assortment of pitchers, bowls, and soup tureens to be used for containers—as if the guests had turned to their own pantries and assembled a casual assortment of what could be found. We then loaded each particular vessel up with enough of one kind of white or blue flowers to show. It was a perfect solution—a casual Sunday supper in perfect harmony with the spirit of the gathering.

We did manage to tuck a little bit of our art into the mix by cutting from luscious white Rieger begonias (the ones with the little dot of egg-yolk yellow in the center of each flower), using jasmine flowers in another, and citrus blossoms and fruit in several others, as well as blue cornflowers, cream-colored French stock, single and double narcissus, and white and lavender lilacs.

Leaving aside issues of the "overhead flower phenomenon," most people want table flowers they can see over. As a rule of thumb, fifteen inches is about as high as you can go, so there is little room left over for a container of any size. Since working in a non-container saves money and allows the savings to be put into the flowers, more often than not we make our centerpieces in inexpensive glass (or plastic) bowls.

Just as you can't plan a menu without first knowing what produce will be fresh and appealing, the idea for the evening's table flowers will come only upon examination of the day's market offerings.

Once you've chosen the flowers you're going to use (presumably the most beautiful ones that could be found on that particular day or the day before), you will already have a good idea of your final result and therefore how to proceed. If you had been moved to buy big brash peonies, lush garden roses, a pot or two of vivid geraniums, and a big handful of purple lilacs, you would

WHEREAS CENTERPIECES made for small tables benefit by adherence to the fifteen-inch rule, guests seated around larger tables rarely talk *across* the table. Therefore tables in excess of five feet can accommodate more sumptuous center arrangements.

A FRIEND of ours recently attended a gala evening at New York's Metropolitan Opera House, and delivered this description of the flowers created for the table centerpieces: "Tall sheaves of wheat crowned with pineapple-shaped masses of 'Casablanca' lilies out of which white and magenta dendrobium orchids shot in all directions. Ghastly," he pronounced, and added that these gigantic concoctions were not only ugly but must have cost a fortune, an idea that displeased him no end, having paid a thousand dollars for his place at the table. Curious as to why events such as these often sport such outlandish flower ideas, he questioned one of the chairpersons of the event. "Do you remember what you ate that night?" she asked. "No," he replied. "Or the wine that was served? Or the music that accompanied the evening?" "Not really," he said, over and over. "Well then," she returned, "I would say that the evening's flowers were a grand success!"

But were they really?

No matter how many you have to make for an occasion, each table centerpiece should look specially made for its own set of guests. To prove the point, here are six—equal but each very different.

WE FREQUENTLY have to make table flowers quickly, in great numbers, and for an affordable price. We usually make up our green bases the day before and add flowers the day of the party. Cutting from plants can save both time and money, for the foliage and flowers of each plant can accomplish a good deal. For instance, using a potted azalea to sketch out a whole centerpiece and to cover the brick of foam gets all the "dirty work" done quickly and provides an appropriate backdrop for the flowers—and all for a reasonable price. This leaves plenty of money for more expensive flowers to finish the job.

Event flowers should never look as if they were concocted by some sort of flower factory, rows and rows of identical mixes. We try to vary each arrangement enough to give it its own individual balance and character while keeping within the overall floral idea of the party.

Before choosing flowers, think of what you want to accomplish. A simple basket of cornflowers sets a more casual and relaxed tone for the coming evening. How much more formal the same setting would feel with a silver bowl of majestic lilies or a compote of champagne roses crowning the table.

be on your way to an opulent centerpiece loaded with sizable, impressive, richly toned flowers. On the other hand, if you were drawn to choose delicate blue cornflowers, tiny white allium, white ranunculus tinged with burgundy edges, narcissus, checkerboard lilies, and grape hyacinths, the end result would definitely be subtle, woodsy-looking, and quietly spread within a range of two colors.

With a block of floral foam carefully taped into place and fully soaked with warm water, you can begin. The first order of business is to "cover" the foam, so that you don't have to worry about trying to hide it later on.

In the first arrangement just described, the final look of the green base hardly matters, for the flowers are the thing and the base will be entirely obscured. Here the geranium leaves, multicolored and patterned like endpapers in a fine book, might be used as if they were a flower—that is to say, featured, not buried underneath.

The second arrangement, however, *depends* on its base, for the small-scale flowers will emerge from it as if growing on a grassy streambank. The foliage therefore is of paramount concern and must be chosen and inserted into the foam with great care.

Small cyclamen leaves might work as a start, combined with excess foliage from the bunches of grape hyacinths and narcissus. Some of the ranunculus flowers will have multiple stems, a few of which will be mostly green leaves and an emerging bud, and these, too, will contribute to the base. If the foliage is pretty, I would buy several extra bunches of cornflowers, for the grasslike stems are perfect to the cause.

Certain plants are ideal for cutting from, whereas others are not. Tulips are useless, for their foliage is unwieldy in this context, as well as being a strange, washed-out color next to most values of green. Ferns are so unrelated to flowers that they don't combine very logically, although in more complicated work that might be an advantage. Use foliage that bears some resemblance to the flowers you have chosen.

We insert foliage in irregular ways to form a somewhat haphazard-looking tangle. Since our centerpieces look different when seen from each individual perspective, the first moves as well as the final ones must be irregular. This is fairly easy when working with foliage cut from plants, for there are usually leaves or branches of different shapes and positions within the same plant. One might be inserted straight up, just off center; a second put in sideways near the bottom edge, so it touches the tablecloth; a third cut much shorter and angling toward two o'clock; and so forth. Hold any flower or leaf between your thumb and forefinger and rotate it—you will soon discover which side is the prettiest, which angle is best, and therefore just how to insert it into the arrangement.

Check each move to see if it works. If it looks odd, try it in another spot or twist it in another direction until it looks better.

Once the block of foam has been hidden, sketch in the arrangement, starting with the most important pieces (often the largest or most striking flowers), turning the container as you work. We like to work just above the counter, setting the dishes on an upside-down clay pot or small plastic bucket so that we can turn them easily and not get tangled up with flowers and discarded trimmings on the counter below. Separating the centerpiece from the debris of the table also allows you to see the outline or shape of the arrangement more readily as you are working, as well as to position a few flowers that will touch the table once the arrangement is set in place.

Try to preserve a sense of space between some of the flowers—think of it as a little breathing room—so that the final creation doesn't look clogged up and crowded. Especially with larger flowers, unless you are purposefully striving for something overdone and blowsy, avoid a heavy touch and try to preserve a feeling of gracefulness and delicacy.

Table flowers are a great opportunity to introduce a little whimsy into your work. We all get a little bit too serious about these matters and here is a chance to rectify that. Look for flowers with a sense of humor, such as coralbells, 'Rip Van Winkle' narcissus, tiny little pineapples, some types of oddly colored ranunculus, tweedia, forget-me-nots, little kalanchoe flowers, and other cuttings from succulents, and add a lighter note or two to the mix. Try to imagine that there will be a number of people sitting around the table, each with a unique view of the flowers.

MAKE SOMETHING NICE FOR EACH OF THEM.

WHEN LEAVES or flower stems are too flexible to be inserted in the foam, make a small opening with a pencil or a smaller pointed instrument and put flowers in the resulting hole.

Since trailing ivy is so widely used for so many floral purposes, we usually pass it by. Many market greens are flat and one-sided, whereas greens cut from small plants are a variety of sizes and shapes. Florist's greens such as branches of huckleberry, lemon leaves, ruscus, or boxwood usually have no visual connection or relationship to the flowers being used, and simply look awkward, ill-placed, and foreign.

AN OPEN LETTER TO FLORISTS

It's not hard to argue that flowers are among the most breathtaking and beautiful elements of the natural universe. They exist in countless forms, in every conceivable place, often growing nobly against insurmountable odds. From this incredible realm of flowers should be found the creative material for the fresh-flower industry—right? **THIS STATEMENT REQUIRES A YES OR NO ANSWER...** consider yours.

We answer an emphatic "yes" to that statement, so it has always astonished us right from the moment we entered the flower business that most professionals have but the most meager examples of this wondrous universe with which to do their work. As you have seen, we have always had to scratch and claw to widen our own range of supplies. As florists and businessmen, we could learn an important lesson from some of our counterparts in the fresh-food and restaurant business. They saw a situation wanting and did something about it.

Whereas twenty years ago there existed a fairly homogeneous selection of markets and restaurants around the country (with a few notable exceptions peppered about in important places), today we all celebrate the availability of an extraordinary range of fresh-food materials, and the most diverse means of preparing and presenting them in almost every city in the land.

Beginning, perhaps, with Julia Child's television antics (which made the vocabulary of haute cuisine comfortable and accessible to millions, and the kitchen a playpen instead of a torture chamber), helped along by Alice Waters' battle cry for only the freshest and most interesting ingredients (down with iceberg lettuce!) and Lee Bailey's beautiful books picturing the rewards of cooking with perfectly fresh, well-chosen produce, and nurtured by two generations of aspiring cooks who have searched the near and far regions of the earth for ideas and returned to combine

them for us in the most captivating ways, goaded on by the food press, a revolution within an industry has taken place—and everyone has emerged a winner.

Consumers everywhere delight in the amazing cooking and eating possibilities, restaurant owners are happy to be intriguing customers once again, and suppliers of the greatly extended range of raw materials continue to multiply, adding more natural ingredients to the markets as time goes on and profiting from the experience.

We florists could learn a lesson from this phenomenon.

It's curious to me that an industry as important to us all as the flower industry has remained pretty much as it was forty or fifty or more years ago. Music and art and theater and literature and film are all on a cultural roller coaster, reflecting the changing times, subject to tremendous artistic license, and mirroring the ever-evolving balance of cultural diversity that is a by-product of our pluralistic society. Flowers, it seems to me, are curiously silent. Perhaps there have been technological advances and innovations, but, looking back on it, not a great deal of excitement

and change has been added to the traditional mix.

While there are, of course, exceptions to these statements, in our travels in many parts of this country and around Europe we have noticed a kind of sameness everywhere, both in what is commercially available to the florist and in what is eventually presented to the customer.

Given the enormous diversity of cultures in the world, as well as the differences in the regions of our own country, and coupled with that the incredible range of flowers that grow in all parts of the globe, this is a most extraordinary situation.

As we see it, here are some of the problems.

The fresh-flower industry everywhere has standardized its creations in order to facilitate its transactions, but in so doing it has drastically narrowed the options and encouraged each practitioner to create a similar product. As we've already stated, this practice is reassuring to those who must know exactly what they're getting or sending, but we feel that it reduces what should be a creative act into a universally acceptable rote exercise.

SOLUTION: *Now is the time when both possibilities can begin to exist side by side, allowing for reassurance for those unwilling or afraid to trust the eye and the art of the practitioner, while encouraging others to explore new possibilities with locally produced materials. Think about it.*

The huge international flower industry is set up to grow the flowers that are in demand around the world. The flowers most in demand are the flowers most often used. Since so many florists are geared up to make a similar product, most order and receive the same materials. (I know that there are lots of exceptions—but the point still stands.) If we agree that one of the wonderful things about fresh flowers is their great variety, we must also recognize that we have created a system that encourages exactly the opposite kind of production.

SOLUTION: *Voice a demand for an extensive array of new choices. Until we create a large enough demand, the markets will remain the way they are and the offerings will remain familiar and limited, forcing dissatisfied consumers to look for alternative sources.*

In our travels, we have observed that many florists who have little recourse to new flower choices—and therefore the possibility of interesting new combinations—update their offerings by concentrating on the "peripherals"—the various accessories that many florists add to flowers to try to make them special for an occasion or to differentiate them from standard offerings. Since we feel strongly that it is the inherent beauty of the flowers themselves that should be given first voice, we feel that this is only sidestepping the problem.

SOLUTION: *Think first of flowers, not ribbons or gimmicks. Vary your offerings and get the markets to help you do it.*

We have made our products too cheap. In our laudable desire to make flowers and floral services affordable to a wide range of customers, we have allowed (or unwittingly encouraged) a perception to develop in the customer's mind that flowers shouldn't cost very much money. A bit like the fast-food franchises, we have often worked with least-common-denominator logic to keep the price of flowers affordable. But just as it is more expensive to prepare meals with perfectly fresh and varied produce, it is more expensive to buy and provide a wide selection of interesting flowers. We have done ourselves a certain disservice by defining our craft as inexpensively as we have, for it has not allowed us the means for growing our businesses and expanding the kinds of beauty we might offer.

An intelligent consumer knows that he must pay appropriately for what he is going to get. If we continue to insist that the only flowers we will carry must bear the burden that flowers must always be inexpensive, we will never be able to expand the repertoire. There is a world of difference between a bunch of cheaply grown pale pink tulips and elegant, long-stemmed, richly colored flaming parrots grown in the south of France. Both are

tulips, but the similarity ends with the name. Whenever possible, there should be room on our shelves for both.

SOLUTION: *Begin to reeducate your customers by offering tantalizing new choices, albeit for more money than the usual ones. And get excited about the possibilities yourself—you'll be amazed how much better your shop looks to you when it's filled with a changing array of eye-catching new alternatives. Give your customer's a real blatant choice—you'll be surprised at what happens.*

When anything is experienced too often, it becomes familiar to us; we just get used to it. It can be food, it can be love-making, it can be flowers. Most of us tire of the same thing and seek out diversity. For instance, although there are those among us who consistently choose the predictability and uniformity of fast-food dining, when most of us eat out, we like to choose from a variety of cuisines we favor in order to experience a wide spectrum of food. Why should flowers be any different?

Like a hamburger or a chicken wing, there is nothing inherently wrong with a carnation, a chrysanthemum, a daisy, or any other variety typically found in a florist's cooler. But these flowers, which have had a ubiquitous presence over the past many years, carry a certain amount of baggage with them. Through no fault of their own they have lost their sense of uniqueness and personality. They've just been overworked and, in some instances, can't cut it anymore. Period.

SOLUTION: *Give the tired ones a rest. Cast about for new possibilities.*

A gift of flowers is meant to stir some-

thing in the heart of the recipient, to make an impact, to carry and convey a personal message from the sender. How can that happen if the flowers sent look and feel too familiar—as if they had been seen and sent many times before?

Look at this issue closely, for if we, as florists, don't fully believe ourselves that the kind of experience an unexpected or tantalizing array of flowers can provide a recipient is wholly different from that offered by a familiar bouquet, we will never be convinced to sell any but the more common varieties.

SOLUTION: *Look to a wide range of fresh-flower choices and learn to combine them in dozens of different ways so that each gift can be specially made.*

THERE IS ROOM in this world for all sorts of opinions and points of view. We recognize that ours is but one voice among many, but we raise it now because we are alarmed at the situation we see. As I traveled across the country on behalf of my first book, I met hundreds of new as well as seasoned florists who echoed many of the concerns I've outlined above, wishing that they could do something about the situation. They can. You can. Strength is found in numbers.

So, as far as we're concerned, the time has come to open our collective doors, sweep the gathered dust off the doorstep, and let a little fresh air wander inside. Let's have at it—it's going to be a hell of a new deal.

FLOWER SOURCES

Caribbean Cuts
120 West 28 Street
New York, NY 10001
212-924-6969 (tel.); 212-967-6975 (fax)
Importers and wholesalers of tropical flowers
and foliage *to the trade only*

Dutch Flower Line
148 West 28 Street
New York, NY 10001
212-727-8600 (tel.); 212-727-7198 (fax)
Importers of premium flowers *to the trade only*

Fischer & Page
134 West 28 Street
New York, NY 10001
212-645-4106 (tel.); 212-645-5440 (fax)
Growers and importers of unusual flowering
material *to the trade only*

Garden Valley Wholesale
707-792-0337 (tel.); 707-792-0349 (fax)
Garden roses from May through November.
Minimum order 60 stems.

La Loma Roses
805-386-8002 (tel.); 805-386-3162 (fax)
Growers and shippers of garden roses *to the
trade only*

Pure Mädderlake products—including floral
arrangements, containers, home furnishings,
and their book *Flowers Rediscovered*—are
available through their store in New York City.
800-304-MADD (tel.).

FLOWER AND HERB CATALOGS [*Suggested by Linda Yang*]

Most of the time I buy the flowers and herbs for my garden at local nurseries. This way I can get the season going quickly with good-sized plants and don't have to wait so long for my harvest and arrangements. Buying locally also means that I can see what I'm really getting in terms of flower or leaf color, texture, and form.

But there are times when the species I hanker for are not available nearby and a mail-order supplier is the only way to go. When buying this way, I prefer to purchase plants that are rooted in soil and grown in pots (as opposed to those with bare roots wrapped in straw). Here's a sampling of some of the many mail-order sources who supply them:

Bluestone Perennials
7211 Middle Ridge Rd.
Madison, OH 44057
800-852-5243

Forestfarm
990 Tetherow Rd.
Williams, OR 97544
503-846-6963

Fox Hill Farm
P.O. Box 9
443 W. Michigan Ave.
Parma, MI 49269
517-531-3179

Holbrook Farm & Nursery
Rt. 2, Box 223 B
Fletcher, NC 28732
704-891-7790

Klehm Nursery
Rt. 5, Box 197
Penny Rd.
South Barrington, IL 60010
800-553-3715

Logee's Greenhouses
141 North St.
Danielson, CT 06239
203-774-8038

Milaeger's Garden
4838 Douglas Ave.
Racine, WI 53402
414-639-2371

Nor'East Miniature Roses
58 Hammond St.
Rowley, MA 01969
508-948-7964

Rosehill Farm
Gregg Neck Rd.
Galena, MD 21635
301-648-5538

The Rosemary House
120 S. Market St.
Mechanicsburg, PA 17055
717-697-5111

Sunnybrook Farms Nursery
P.O. Box 6
9448 Mayfield Rd.
Chesterland, OH 44026
216-729-7232

Taylor's Herb Gardens
1535 Lone Oak Rd.
Vista, CA 92084
619-727-3485

We-Du Nurseries
Rt. 5, Box 724
Marion, NC 28752
704-738-8300

Well-Sweep Herb Farm
317 Mt. Bethel Rd.
Port Murray, NJ 07865
908-852-5390

White Flower Farm
Rt. 63
Litchfield, CT 06759
203-496-9600

Linda Yang writes for the New York
Times *and is the author of* The City
Gardener's Handbook: From Balcony
to Backyard

FURTHER READING [*Suggested by Timothy Mawson*]

The following list offers a wide selection of books on flower arranging: the history of flower decoration and general books on flower painters, an inspirational source for flower arrangers. However, most are out of print, but with some effort and patience can be obtained through secondhand and antiquarian bookdealers.

Ashberry, A. *Miniature Flowers & Vases* (1955)

Bazin, G. *A Gallery of Flowers* (1960)

Berrall, J. S. *A History of Flower Arrangement* (1953)

Brotherston, R. P. *The Book of Cut Flowers* (1906)

Burbridge, F. W. *Domestic Floriculture— Window Gardening & Floral Decorations, Being Practical Directions for the Propagation, Culture & Arrangement of Plants & Flowers as Domestic Ornaments* (1874)

Clements, J. *Fun with Flowers—A Treatise on the Art of Flower Arrangement* (1952)

Edwards, N. De Kalb. *The Art of Flower Arrangement* (1964)

Emberton, S. *Garden Foliage for Flower Arrangement* (1970)

———. *Shrub Gardening for Flower Arrangement* (1973)

Felton, R. F. *British Floral Decoration* (1910)

Hulton, P. & Smith, L. *Flowers in Art—From East & West* (1974)

Jekyll, Gertrude. *Flower Decoration in the House* (1907)

Kent, E. *Flora Domestica or the Portable Flower Garden, with Directions for the Treatment of Plants in Pots* (1831)

Kittel, M. B. *Japanese Flower Arrangement* (1961)

MacQueen, Sheila. *Encyclopedia of Flower Arranging* (1967)

Madderlake. *Flowers Rediscovered* (1985)

March, Penny J. *The Master's Book of Ikebana* (1976)

Mitchell, P. *European Flower Painters* (1973)

Nichols, Beverly. *The Art of Flower Arrangement* (1968)

Preininger, M. *Japanese Flower Arrangement— For Modern Homes* (1936)

Pulbrook & Gould. *The Pulbrook & Gould Book of Flower Arrangement* (1947)

Rockwell, F. F. & Grayson, E. C. *The Complete Book of Flower Arrangement* (1947)

Sadler, A. I. *The Art of Flower Arrangement in Japan—A Sketch of Its History & Development* (1933)

Sato, Shozo. *The Art of Arranging Flowers—A Complete Guide to Japanese Ikebana* (1975)

Scrouse, N. *The Art & Science of Flowers* (1973)

Smith, G. *Flower Arranging in House & Garden* (1977)

———. *George Smith's Flower Decoration* (1988)

Sparon, N. J. *Japanese Arrangement—Classical & Modern* (1960)

Spry, Constance. *Flower Decoration* (1934)

———. *Flowers in the House & Garden* (1937)

———. *Garden Notebook* (1940)

———. *Winter & Spring Flowers* (1951)

———. *Summer & Autumn* (1951)

———. *A Constance Spry Anthology* (1953)

———. *How to Do the Flowers* (1953)

———. *Party Flowers* (1953)

———. *Flower Favorites* (1959)

Stevenson, V. *The Encyclopedia of Floristry* (1953)

Teshigahara, S. *Sofu—His Boundless World of Flowers & Form* (1966)

Timothy Mawson is a bookseller in New Preston, Connecticut, specializing in new and antiquarian garden books.

INDEX

PHOTOGRAPH CREDITS

LANGDON CLAY 1, 3, 4-5, 7, 9, 14, 15, 19, 24, 26, 28, 34 *(left),* 44, 45, 48, 49, 51, 52, 53, 54, 55, 56, 57, 58, 60, 61, 62, 66 *(bottom),* 73, 74, 75, 76, 77, 78, 79, 80, 81, 85, 86, 88, 92, 93, 94 *(top right),* 95, 96, 97, 98, 99, 100, 101, 102, 103, 104, 107, 108, 109, 112, 113, 114, 115, 117, 121, 122, 123 *(center),* 127, 132, 133, 134, 135, 136, 139, 155, 156-157, 158 *(left),* 159, 161 *(right),* 162 *(right),* 164,165 *(right),* 166, 174, 178, 180, 181, 186-87, 188, 189, 190-91

MICHAEL GEIGER 70 *(bottom),* 123 *(top right),* 129, 140, 185

BRIAN HAGIWARA 91 *(bottom)*

TOM PRITCHARD 2, 6, 8, 10, 11, 13, 16, 17, 18, 20, 21, 22, 23, 25, 27, 29, 30, 31, 33, 34 *(right),* 35, 36, 37, 38, 40, 41, 42, 43, 46, 47, 61 *(top),* 63, 64-65, 66 *(top),* 67, 68, 70-71, 72, 82, 83, 87, 89, 90, 91 *(top and middle),* 94 *(left and bottom right),* 105, 106, 110, 111, 118, 119, 120, 123 *(top left and bottom),* 124, 125, 128, 129, 131, 138, 141, 143, 144, 145, 146, 147, 148, 149, 150, 151, 152, 153, 154, 158 *(right),* 160, 161 *(left),* 162 *(left),* 163, 165 *(left),* 167, 168, 169, 170, 171, 172, 173, 176, 192